Radical Universalism

Are All Religions the Same?

Sri Dharma Pravartaka Acharya

Radical Universalism

Are All Religions the Same?

Sri Dharma Pravartaka Acharya

ISDS

Omaha, NE, USA

2024

International Sanatana Dharma Society

13917 P Street

Omaha, NE 68137

© Copyright 2024, International Sanatana Dharma Society

All rights reserved. No part of this book may be reproduced or utilized in any form or by any means, electronic or mechanical, including photocopying, recording, or by any information storage and retrieval system, without permission in writing from the publisher.

www.dharmacentral.com

Other Works by Sri Dharma Pravartaka Acharya

Sanatana Dharma: The Eternal Natural Way

The Sanatana Dharma Study Guide

The Dharma Manifesto

The Vedic Way of Knowing God

Living Dharma: The Teachings of Sri Dharma Pravartaka Acharya

Radical Universalism: Are All Religions the Same?

Taking Refuge in Dharma: The Initiation Guidebook

The Shakti Principle: Encountering the Feminine Power of God

Introduction to Sanatana Dharma

Principles of Perfect Leadership

Interregnum: Restoring Authentic Rulership in the Kali Yuga

Be Strong: The Vedic Guide to Self-Empowerment

Lord of the Rings, Dharma and Modernity

The Vedic Encyclopedia

Narada Bhakti Sutras: Translation and Commentary

Vedanta: The Culmination of Wisdom

The Dharma of Wellbeing

Jnana Yoga: The Art of Wisdom

The Dharma Dialogues

Isha Upanishad: Translation and Commentary

Audio

Mantra Meditations (CD)

All these works can be purchased at:
www.dharmacentral.com

Table of Contents

Chapter One: Radical Universalism –
An Anti-Vedic Dogma 11

Chapter Two: A Tradition of Consideration,
Not Capitulation 25

Chapter Three: The Distinctively Unique
Vedic Religion 31

Chapter Four: Letting the Tradition Speak
for Itself 37

Chapter Five: Clearly Defining
Sanatana Dharma 45

Chapter Six: Dharma Rakshakas: The Defenders
of Dharma 57

Chapter Seven: Traditional Sanatana Dharma
Versus Modern Neo-Hinduism 63

Chapter Eight: The Dogmas of
Neo-Hinduism 73

Chapter Nine: The Non-Vedic Origins of
Radical Universalism 123

Chapter Ten: Logical Fallacies of Radical

Universalism 145

Chapter Eleven: Radical Universalism and
Ethical Relativism 153

Chapter Twelve: Sanatana Dharma –
The Empty Mirror? 169

Chapter Thirteen: Brahman – The Absolute of
the Vedas 183

Chapter Fourteen: Distinguishing
Salvific States 193

Chapter Fifteen: My God is Bigger Than
Your God 197

Chapter Sixteen: One God/Many Names –
An Exegetical Analysis of Rig Veda, 1.164.46 ... 205

Chapter Seventeen: Radical Universalism and
Vedic Epistemology 215

Chapter Eighteen: Radical Universalism,
Christian Missionaries and the RSS 219

Chapter Nineteen: Reclaiming the Jewel
of Dharma 231

About the Author 237

Dedication

The present work is dedicated in its entirety to His Divine Grace A.C. Bhaktivedanta Swami Prabhupada, the greatest religious traditionalist, restorer of pure and authentic Dharma, and Vedic Acharya of the 20th Century. This book is dedicated to completing an important portion of the work that he began.

Endorsements by Eminent Vedic Leaders

"Few have the background and fewer still the courage to speak boldly about the unfortunate ascension in modern times of Hindu universalism. Sri Dharma Pravartaka Acharya has both, and wields them in this book to trenchant purpose. Anyone seeking to comprehend the origins and intellectual dangers of an "all religions are the same" mind-set need look no further. It's all flayed open here, logically and compellingly."

- Paramacharya Palaniswami
Editor-in-Chief
Hinduism Today Magazine

"A number of modern spiritual teachers, particularly in the Hindu tradition, in an attempt to be tolerant and inclusive, have made the blanket statement that all religions are true, valid and equal and lead to the same goal. While one should certainly be tolerant and respectful of the existence of different points of view in the spiritual realm just as in the social, political and intellectual spheres, this does not require that we must give up discrimination in the process. Religion is as diverse as any other aspect of life and also contains the high and the low, the good and the bad, and various doctrines that cannot all be equally true. We cannot accept all religions as true any more than we can accept all scientific theories as correct. Such a process puts an end to real inquiry and our ability to discover what is really valid.

Religion, properly speaking, should be a quest for eternal truth and a seeking to realize it within our own consciousness. This requires that we question everything and only accept what is proved by our own experience. For example, the law of karma and rebirth is either true or it is not. If it is true then religions which do not teach it are flawed. If it is not true, then the religions that teach it are incorrect. But both cannot be true at the same time.

The problem is that this radical universalism of all religions being the same has caused Hindus to lose their discrimination about religion. It makes them vulnerable to conversion by keeping them ignorant of important theological and philosophical differences that do exist between Hinduism and other religions and cannot be glossed over.

In his critique of radical universalism, Sri Dharma Pravartaka Acharya has boldly addressed this complex issue with depth, clarity, comprehensiveness and sensitivity and, most importantly, with a profound rationality based upon the great principles of Vedanta. He shows how the Hindu tradition does not teach such a blind equation of all religions, but instead emphasizes an enlightened pluralism that not only allows for the existence of many paths but insists that only a path as sharp as the edge of a razor can take us to the highest goal. There can be no compromise about truth if one wants to realize the Divine Self within, which is the real aim of all religious and spiritual striving. Sri Acharyaji restores this older and deeper approach of the Hindu mind which combines tolerance with truthfulness, and insists upon a philosophical clarity to one's views, regardless of whether others might agree or not.

It is time for Hindus to reexamine this view that all religions are the same, and recognize that what their religion teaches is often different from the teachings of other religions and grants Hinduism a unique beauty, power and wisdom of its own. Yet even beyond this, Hindus should look to find out what is true in religion, whether it requires questioning the doctrines of their own or any other religion. The current book is a good place to begin this transformation that can change the nature of both the individual and the society.

Yet this book is not only relevant to Hindus but to all those who want to know what religion is really all about and where it should take us. It is time for us to move beyond religion as blind faith to an experiential spirituality through which we can discover the entire universe within our own consciousness, beyond all names, forms and personalities. This is what Hinduism really teaches, not that all religions are the same, but that the essence of our Being is one, regardless of outer differences, in which all separate religious identities dissolve into the eternal Dharma."

- Dr. David Frawley (Pandit Vamadeva Shastri)

"Radical Universalism" by Sri Dharma Pravartaka Acharya is an important book that dispels many misconceptions about the Hindu tradition. Sanatana Dharma emphatically speaks of the difference between the asuric and the daivika currents of reality and the need to choose the latter if one wishes to obtain knowledge and understanding. Sri Acharyaji is right to stress that the slogan that "all religions are the same" is antithetical to the spirit of the Vedas. Progress, at the personal and the societal levels, comes only through a process of churning. I recommend this book very strongly."

- Professor Subhash Kak

Author of *"The Prajna Sutra, The Astronomical Code of the Ṛgveda"*, and many other books.

"The book *Radical Universalism* provides some necessary and essential insights and observations that should be familiar material for anyone who understands the difficulties that the modern Vedic society is facing. It brings to light issues that have long been overlooked, or even dismissed, by those that follow Vedic Dharma. I commend Sri Dharma Pravartaka Acharya for being bold enough to state the facts and report on issues that we who have been working to preserve and protect Vedic culture have been dealing with for years. He shows how to lead the conscience of a broader or even global Vedic community in its need to act together to promote to the world a better understanding of Vedic Dharma. I highly recommend that all followers of Vedic Dharma, and those who simply appreciate it, take to heart what Sri Dharma Pravartaka Acharya has to say in this book."

- Stephen Knapp
President of the Vedic Friends Association
Author of over 30 books on Vedic culture and philosophy

"There is nothing like gripping the tail of a tiger and giving it a good shake to start your day off right! Sri Acharyaji's book pins the tail on the donkey...and the donkey is us - those of us who have taken the holy vows of sannyasi are presented with a dunda in order to protect the Vedas. As the book so eloquently points out, Hinduism is in no need of a Neo-Hinduism. Having read Sri Acharyaji's book, it gives me hope that others may celebrate Hinduism in its original form. In knowing the original form in clear and understandable terms, it would be difficult to stay out of that divine intoxication that is our birthright as human beings and has been around in verbal and written form for thousands of years...The Vedas, "Aham Brahmasmi" (I am Brahman). I highly recommend this book and the eternal understanding that it brings."

- H.H. Mahamandaleshwar Swarupananda Vishwa Guru Swami (Ph.D., M.A., Ph.D.)

"In the last two centuries the stalwarts of 'Neo-Hinduism' have confused Hindu tolerance with the belief that 'all religions are same'. Sri Dharma Pravartaka Acharya shows that this belief is not just factually and logically untenable, it also contradicts traditional Hinduism which clearly distinguishes between its own family of traditions and alien belief systems. Acharyaji argues that this 'sameness of all religions' dogma has caused immense harm to Hindus themselves in many ways, and has earned them ridicule and animosity from members of other rival religions such as Islam and Christianity.

In conjunction with a refutation of this Neo-Hindu dogma, Acharyaji provides a succinct and cogent description of core Hindu traditions and beliefs and contrasts them with those of other religions. The 'all religions are same and equal' belief is a mere delusion. Hindus would do well to read Acharyaji's book carefully and extricate themselves from their self-inflicted intellectual stupor."

- Vishal Agarwal (Voice of Dharma)

"Sri Dharma Pravartaka Acharya has kindly broken ranks with many so-called Neo-Hindus by defining in more relevant terms the crux of the Vedic teachings and how it has been compromised by religious icons born in India but corrupted by alien ideas. This has resulted in debasing the original pristine philosophy of the *Vedas* and producing what is now a hodge-podge of a belief system. To rectify this situation Sri Acharyaji has used his analytical talents to convince us otherwise.

A Hindu must know his religion is really Sanatana Dharma, based on eternal religious principles and be proud to follow it and present it, as it is."

- Sripad B.V. Avadhuta Maharaja (Sannyasi of the Gaudiya Sampradaya)

"Hindus living in a modern environment are faced with a problem more unsettling than the physical onslaughts that their civilization has survived. It is an existential crisis: they are no longer sure about the need to continue their ancestral religion. Many of their own religious leaders are telling them that the values and practices of their own tradition are "not Hindu but universal", an assertion they share with non-Hindu exploiters of pieces of Hindu heritage such as yoga. Using seductive metaphors, like the mountain where all paths lead to the same summit, these leaders effectively deny that there is any good reason to be a Hindu rather than Christian or Muslim, teaching instead that "all religions are essentially the same.

"In this book, Dharma teacher Sri Dharma Pravartaka Acharya (American-born Dr. Frank Morales) develops a cogent argument against the universalistic fallacy. He traces its origins in the colonial condition, when prominent Hindus interiorized this novel European idea, and documents its lightning career through divergent sections of Hindu society including such seeming antagonists as Gandhism and Hindu nationalism. He draws attention to the odd sense of superiority which some preachers derive from the allegedly Hindu teaching that "unlike other religions, Hinduism doesn't claim to be unlike other religions". Then he proceeds to deconstruct this fashionable rhetoric about the equal truth of all religions. With compelling logic, he shows its contradictions as well as its undesirable ethical implications. Not least, he proves that it is deeply un-Hindu, for Hinduism values truth over syrupy and futile attempts to please everyone."

- Dr. Koenraad Elst, Belgian Indologist

"This book forthrightly shatters the modern myth that the practitioners of Sanatana Dharma believe in and promote the view that all religions are the same. It is required reading for anyone who seeks the authentic. Sri Dharma Pravartaka Acharya is one of a small, but growing number who are speaking out about the common misperceptions and outright distortions of these ancient traditions and teachings, while personally cultivating the tranquility of an adept."

- Dandi Swami Jnaneshvara Bharati

Foreword

There is a common religious urge in all human beings – a seeking to contact the Divine or a higher spiritual reality – which has had different expressions according to time, place, culture and individual. While there is a common root to our religious seeking and much shared in religious experiences at a mystical level, one also finds a bewildering variety of beliefs and practices in existing religions, so much so that what may be regarded as holy in one tradition may be considered as unholy or unpardonable in another. Because of these differences of thought and action, religion has often led not to unity between human beings but to disagreements, hatred, war and even genocide – a sad phenomenon which does not seem to be decreasing in the current global age of mass communication.

In an effort to be tolerant and inclusive aimed at reducing such conflicts, a number of modern spiritual teachers, particularly in the Hindu tradition, have made the blanket statement that all religions are true, valid and equal and lead to the same goal – what could be called a 'radical universalism'. This radical universalism promotes an acceptance of all religions as the same in order to lead us to the unity behind our religious striving. It gives us the impression that it does not matter what religion one follows, or whether one goes to a church, mosque or temple. One need only give full faith in the religion that one's culture or community has adopted and one can reach the highest truth.

The problem with this view is that it does not remove the actual differences and conflicts that exist between religions, or even seek to resolve them, but pretends they do not really exist and so can be just brushed aside. Not surprisingly, instead of going away, these conflicts continue and lead people not to unity but to conflict.

This general equation of all religions as true, well-intentioned though it may be, gives the impression that religions with all their various dogmas and assertions should be accepted as they are. It is like sanctifying all the borders between nations as valid and then seeking a harmony between the peoples of the world.

Radical universalism can cut off meaningful examination and dialogue as to what constitutes the nature of Truth. Sometimes it places a kind of a taboo on critical examination of religion, as if anything called a religion or any article of religious faith must be accepted without scrutiny. It suggests the equation of religious theologies and philosophies that have not only historical differences, but major differences of view, goal and approach.

While one should certainly be tolerant and respectful of different points of view in the spiritual realm just as in social, political and intellectual spheres, this does not require that we give up discrimination in the process. Nor will such a giving up of discrimination lead to any higher truth that can resolve our conflicts into a real and enduring unity.

Religion is as diverse and multifarious as any domain of human life, perhaps even more so. This is because religion introduces absolutes into human thought that can be divisive and extreme in their consequences. While the religious urge has much that is wonderful in it, it also can be suppressed, distorted or perverted like any other human urge. All these faces of religion may not be true or ennobling to the spirit as history has so often proved.

The different religions of the world contain various doctrines and teachings that cannot all be equally valid. We cannot accept all religious teachings as true any more than we can accept all scientific theories as correct. For example, the law of karma and rebirth is either true or it is not. If it is true, then religions which do not teach it are flawed. If it is not true, then the religions that teach it are incorrect. But both cannot be true at the same time.

Similarly, there can be no final guru, prophet or savior for all humanity, any more than there can be any final scientist, artist or politician. To accept religious claims of exclusivism as valid will only serve to reinforce existing differences, not resolve them into a higher unity.

Religion, in its real import, should be a quest for eternal Truth and a seeking to realize it within our own consciousness. This requires that we question everything and only accept what is proved by our own experience. An adaptation of radical universalism has caused many Hindus to lose their discrimination about religion. It makes them vulnerable to conversion by keeping them ignorant of important theological and philosophical differences that do exist between Hinduism and other religious systems and must take those who believe in them and practice them in very different directions.

One should certainly respect freedom of religion and honor pluralism in the field of religion just as in the domains of science and politics. But one need not mindlessly equate all religions in order to do this. Hindu Dharma teaches us that there is One Truth but many paths. But it does not teach us that all paths lead to that One Truth. There are paths that lead to falsehood or half-truth. Nor are all paths the same. Each path has different guidelines, even if it might reach the same goal. Nor is everything, even in religion, a path to truth but may reflect some other motivation. Hindu dharma teaches us pluralism relative to the spiritual life, which can both tolerate many different points of view but also discriminate between them and find out what is best for each individual.

An enlightened pluralism must rest upon a higher sense of discrimination. That one has pluralism in the variety of food that one can choose from, for example, does not mean that all food is good and one's dietary choices do not have consequences. The same is true of religion. It does matter what one follows in terms of religion because its theology, belief and values will shape one's life and behavior accordingly. A religious system that does not teach an experiential spiritual path to self-realization or God-realization cannot take us there, regardless of whatever else it may have to offer. Religion is a field in which we need the greatest discrimination because it concerns the highest values and deepest core beliefs that shape our lives.

In his insightful book, *Radical Universalism: Are All Religions the Same?,* Sri Dharma Pravartaka Acharya has boldly addressed this complex issue with depth, clarity, comprehensiveness and sensitivity. Most importantly, he bases his views on a profound rationality reflecting the great principles of Vedanta, which insists upon a clear analysis and understanding of the issue, not just the imposition of a belief as the answer.

Perhaps as a westerner who has adapted Hindu Dharma, Sri Acharyaji can show native born Hindus how to communicate their religion to the western world. It is curious to note that in spite of (or perhaps because of) the Hindu idea that all religions are equal; none of the other major world religions today accepts the Hindu religion as valid. On the contrary, the same old ideas of Hinduism as primitive, polytheistic, superstitious and oppressive are commonly echoed by the other religions of the world, as well as in academia and the media. This suggests that it might be better for Hindus to clarify what Hinduism actually teaches rather than be content with saying that Hinduism accepts the teachings of the other religions as well (implying that there is nothing wrong for these religions to denigrate Hinduism, if that is what they want to do).

Sri Dharma Pravartaka Acharya is not content merely to make statements that make everyone feel good about what they already believe in but challenges the reader to look deeper. He shows how the Hindu tradition does not teach a blind equation of all religions, but instead emphasizes an enlightened pluralism that not only allows for the existence of many paths but insists that only a path as sharp as the edge of a razor can take us to the highest goal. There can be no compromise about Truth if one wants to realize the Divine Self within, which is the real aim of all religious and spiritual striving according to the Hindu view. Hindus must reclaim this intellectual clarity if they want to find the real Truth of their religion or of any religion.

In his work, Sri Acharyaji is not trying to criticize any group or teacher in the Hindu tradition or their intentions. It is the lack of intellectual clarity and the corresponding confusion in thought and action that he addresses. Most importantly, he shows how Hindu youth are confused because of this idea that there is nothing in Hinduism that is not also found in other religions. Young Hindus are taught to blindly accept Christianity and Islam as the same as Hinduism, not by preachers from these other religions but by their own Hindu teachers, which makes them vulnerable to conversion. After all, if Christianity and Islam are nothing different, why should one remain a Hindu if there are other incentives to change one's religion?

Such an equation of religions does not equip Hindus with the intellectual skills necessary to express, defend or even share their religion in the global context. It turns Hinduism into a me-too religion that lacks any character, uniqueness or compelling reason to practice or support it. Instead of learning the great teachings and history of Hindu Dharma, Hindus are taught that their religion is just part of a greater urge which other communities have addressed in equally valid ways. Yet when Hindus go to the teachings of other religions, they commonly find dogmas and doctrines that aim to destroy their regard for their own tradition.

It is time for Hindus to reexamine this view of radical universalism that all religions are the same, and recognize that what their religion teaches is often different from the teachings of other religions and grants Hinduism a unique beauty, power and wisdom. Yet beyond this, Hindus should look to find out what is true in religion, whether it requires questioning the doctrines of their own religion or any other religion. The current book is a good place to begin this necessary transformation.

Yet the book is not only relevant to Hindus but to all those who want to know what religion is really about and where it should take us. It is time for us to move beyond religion as blind faith to an experiential spirituality through which we can discover the entire universe within our own consciousness, beyond all names, forms and personalities. This is what Hinduism really teaches, not that all religions are the same, but the essence of our Being is One, regardless of all outer differences.

Dr. Frank Morales (Ph.D.) has taken the Hindu name Dharma Pravartaka Acharya or "the one who teaches and establishes Dharma." Unlike most westerners who embrace various Hindu-based teachings according to one guru or lineage only, he looks to the tradition as a whole, its universal relevance and how to promote it in the modern world. Notably, Sri Dharma Pravartaka Acharya has become the first western born Acharya for a Hindu temple in North America. In this regard, he is creating an important role model for future generations of Hindus.

Sri Acharyaji has many other writings that are relevant in the study of religion and in the application of spiritual practices. I would encourage the reader to examine these as well. Most importantly, Hindus should follow his inspiration to work to uphold Sanatana Dharma (the eternal teachings behind Hinduism) both in its unique essence and in its universal grasp.

Then there cannot only be a revival of Hindu Dharma but of Dharma as a whole for a peace and understanding in the world that can allow religion and spirituality to flower in every possible way.

Dr. David Frawley (Pandit Vamadeva Shastri)
Santa Fe, New Mexico USA
November 2007

Introduction

The anti-Vedic craze of Radical Universalism first began to influence traditional Sanatana Dharma roughly 200 years ago as a direct result of liberal Christian missionary and Euro-American, globalist ideological incursions into India. Since then, it has morphed to become one of the most perniciously parroted dogmas in modern-day Hinduism[1] to the point where, today, many people throughout the world – not the least of whom seem to be a

---

[1] There are two separate terms used throughout this book: "Sanatana Dharma" versus "Neo-Hinduism". They point to two very different religious phenomena. The term Sanatana Dharma designates the original, unaltered and authentic Vedic tradition, which is based upon the actual teachings of the Vedic scriptures and the ancient *rishis*. Neo-Hinduism, which means literally "New Hinduism", on the other hand, is the very modern, subverted caricature of Sanatana Dharma that came about in the very early 19th century as a result of the interface of the Vedic tradition with modernity. Sanatana Dharma is not merely another synonymous term for Neo-Hinduism. The two words are not merely dual terms for the same religion. One actually has little to do with the other. Radical Universalism is a phenomenon found exclusively in modern Neo-Hinduism, and not in authentic Sanatana Dharma.

majority of the Hindu population - falsely believe the dogma of Radical Universalism to be a central pillar of Sanatana Dharma itself. While a handful of responsible and honest *gurus* and Hindu intellectuals have made courageous attempts to negate this anti-Vedic fallacy over the last two centuries, few have succeeded in formulating a concerted and systematic philosophical response. This work presently represents the first such successful philosophical critique and refutation of Radical Universalism in the history of Sanatana Dharma.

When I first published this work as a long essay in November of 2003, I knew that many of the concepts presented here would be relatively unknown and seemingly novel to many of today's Vedic readers and leaders, this despite their conjectural grounding in both Vedic scriptures and in the teachings of the *rishis*, *acharyas*, and systematizers of traditional Vedic and Vedantic philosophy over the course of the last 5,000 years. I also anticipated that there would be some amount of controversy and passionate discussion of this work for precisely this reason. What I did not anticipate, however, was the precise magnitude of readership, coverage, and debate that this work would ultimately instigate.

By 2007, four short years after its initial publication, "*Radical Universalism*" had been read by over one-million people, including many of the most important Hindu/Vedic leaders on Earth. It had appeared in a dozen print journals (including as a feature article in *Hinduism Today* magazine, the largest Hindu publication on earth), had been reproduced in multiple hundreds of websites and Hinduism discussion forums globally, and had been translated into several languages.

While I am certainly humbled and happy with the enormous response that my work has generated in the last few years, I have also been somewhat bewildered by the lack of understanding on the part of a small number of readers that I have periodically seen about the precise nature and purpose of this work. It has been to hopefully alleviate some of these misunderstandings that I have decided to publish this expanded edition of my "*Radical Universalism*" work.

While there have been many readers of my work, there has also been an unfortunate degree of mistaken notions about what this work is precisely about. The thesis of this work is a relatively simple one: The claim of Radical Universalism that "*all religions are the same*" is not a claim that is upheld anywhere in traditional Sanatana Dharma, is not a claim that is Vedic in origin at all, and is a claim that is contrary to logic, reason, common sense, Vedic Shastra (scripture) and *pramana* (valid means of Vedic epistemic inquiry), and is thus a claim that is rendered wholly absurd in retrospect of thorough analysis.

The vast majority of readers - both lay-readers, as well as contemporary Vedic leaders and scholars alike - seem to have been in general agreement with the grounding thesis of this work upon examining it. A small minority of individuals, however, initially resisted the work. This latter reaction seems to have been due to several factors, including only reading the beginning portion of the work - which is the easier-to-read, historical grounding of the origins of Radical Universalism - without then proceeded to the more important and challenging philosophical section; or making the erroneous mistake of thinking that I was minimizing one or two well-known historical figures in Neo-Hinduism (literally, the "New Hinduism"),[2] rather than attacking an

---

[2] The academically accepted term "Neo-Hinduism" points specifically to the very modern trend within "Hinduism" that

overarching fallacy that has become a part of modern day Neo-Hinduism; or generally not being able to follow the challenging philosophical arguments that the work was outlining.

Today, fortunately, even most of these original detractors have come to quietly revise their initial opinions and objections, and have now joined wholeheartedly in the cause to support authentic, traditionalist Sanatana Dharma against the anti-Vedic onslaught of Radical Universalism.

---

is predicated upon a) Radical Universalism, b) the acceptance of the modern scientific world-view over and above the world-view of the Vedic scriptures, c) the acceptance of kathenotheism (the idea that all gods are interchangeable), d) the equation of being of Indian descent as synonymous with being a "Hindu", or a follower of Sanatana Dharma, e) the *via negativa* definition of being "Hindu" as not being Muslim, among other commonly held, non-Vedic dogmas. Tragically, a slight majority of Indian Hindus today are consciously or unconsciously following Neo-Hindu dogmas rather than the pure teachings of scripturally-based Sanatana Dharma.

My goal in presenting *Radical Universalism* in book form is precisely to help the Vedic world in its present attempt to reconstruct itself in terms of its ancient and time-honored form. If we are to call ourselves either Vedic or followers of Sanatana Dharma, and if we are going to express our heart-felt concern that our beautiful and noble tradition successfully rebuild itself to become a future force for global renaissance, then we need to understand the true nature of this dignified and life-sustaining spiritual world-view in a manner that honors it in an unadulterated and pristine manner. We need to understand the tradition of Sanatana Dharma on its own terms and on its terms alone, and not under the terms of its detractors and enemies.

As one of India's premiere publishers of books on Hinduism, Dharma, and South Asian Studies, it is with gratitude that I acknowledge Voice of India's dedication to publishing the Indian edition, the very first edition, of this book. With the 2024 second edition of this important book, it is also my fervent hope that this work can continue to make some contribution to the continued revival of authentic Sanatana Dharma as a global force for positive and constructive change in our world today.

Aum Hari Aum,

Sri Dharma Pravartaka Acharya
President-Acharya
International Sanatana Dharma Society
December 1, 2007
Revised for Second Edition, December 1, 2023

Acknowledgements

I want to thank the following people for their inspiration, encouragement, and continued personal support for my work over the years.

Param Pujya Sri Swami Dayananda Sarasvati, His Holiness Sri Bodhinatha Veylanswami, Dr. David Frawley, Dr. Subhash Kak, Steven Knapp, H.H. Mahamandaleshwar Swarupananda Swami, Sripad B.V. Avadhuta Maharaja, Tulasi Devi, Mr. AJ Hoge, Professor Keith Yandell, Professor David M. Knipe, Vishal Agarwal, and Professor Ramesh Rao.

Special thanks to Tulasi Devi Mandaleshvari for her creative expertise in designing the cover for this book. Thank you to Marc König, Tim Heibach and Krishna Prasada and Savitri Devi for your expert proofreading, as well as to Hayagriva for heading up the ISDS book publishing team.

Chapter One: Radical Universalism – An Anti-Vedic Dogma

It is by no means an exaggeration to say that the ancient religion of Sanatana Dharma has been one of the least understood religious traditions in the history of world religion. The sheer number of stereotypes, misconceptions, and outright false notions about what Sanatana Dharma teaches, as well as about the precise practices and behavior that it asks of its followers, out-number those of any other religion currently known combined. Leaving the more obviously grotesque crypto-colonialist caricatures of cow-worshipping, caste domination and "sutee" aside, even many of the most fundamental theological and philosophical foundations of Sanatana Dharma often remain inexplicable mysteries to the general public and supposed scholars of "Hindu Studies".

More disturbing, however, is the fact that many wild misconceptions about the beliefs of Sanatana Dharma are prevalent even among the bulk of purported followers of the Vedic tradition and, alarmingly, even to many purportedly learned spiritual teachers, *gurus*, and *swamis* who claim to lead the religion in present times.

Of the many current peculiar concepts mistakenly ascribed to Vedic theology, one of the most widely misunderstood is the idea that Sanatana Dharma somehow teaches that all religions are equal…that all religions are the same, with the same purpose, goal, experientially tangible salvific state, and object of ultimate devotion. So often has this notion been thoughtlessly repeated by so many - from the common Hindu parent to the latest *swamiji* arriving on American shores yearning for a popular following - that it has now become artificially transformed into a supposed foundation stone of modern Hindu teachings. Many modern-day followers of Sanatana Dharma are now completely convinced that this is actually what Sanatana Dharma teaches.

Despite its widespread popular repetition, however, does Sanatana Dharma actually teach the idea that all religions are really the same? Even a cursory examination of the very long history of Vedic philosophical thought, as well as an objective analysis of the ultimate logical implications of such a nonsensical proposition, quickly makes it quite apparent that traditional Sanatana Dharma has never supported such an idea.

The doctrine of what I have come to call "Radical Universalism" makes the claim that "*all religions are the same.*" This dogmatic assertion is of very recent origin, and has become one of the most harmful misconceptions in the Vedic world in the last 200 or so years. It is a doctrine that has directly led to a self-defeating philosophical/theological relativism that has, in turn, weakened the stature and dignity of Sanatana Dharma to its very core. The doctrine of Radical Universalism has made Vedic philosophy look infantile in the eyes of non-Dharmis,[3] has led to a collective state of self-revulsion, confusion, and shame in the minds of too many Hindu youth, and has opened the Hindu community to be preyed upon much more easily by the zealous missionaries of other religions, specifically the Abrahamic religions.[4]

---

[3] The only proper and correct term for a follower of Sanatana Dharma is the word "Dharmi", or "one who adheres to Dharma". The terms "Sanatani" and "Hindu" are of very modern creation, linguistically inaccurate and thus meaningless terms.

[4] The major Abrahamic religions are Judaism, mainstream Christianity and Islam. All three of these very aggressive religions have made inroads into the Vedic world and have forcefully converted many to their respective religions. The doctrine of Radical Universalism has been one of the many tools at the disposal of Abrahamist missionaries in their concerted attempt to destroy the last remnants of Dharma in the world.

The problem of Radical Universalism is arguably the most important philosophical issue facing the global Vedic community today. Moreso than any anti-Vedic incursion threatening Sanatana Dharma from without, Radical Universalism has been responsible for subverting Sanatana Dharma from within. In the following book, we will perform an in-depth examination of the intrinsic fallacies contained in this inherently anti-Vedic idea, as well as the untold damage that Radical Universalism has wrought in Sanatana Dharma, and especially in the more modern offshoot of Sanatana Dharma known as "Hinduism".

What's a Kid to Do?

Indian Hindu parents, very specifically, are to be given immense credit. The daily challenges that typical Hindu parents face in encouraging their children to maintain their commitment to the Vedic tradition are enormous and very well-known. These

Hindu parents try their best to observe some fidelity to the religion of their ancestors, often having little understanding of the religion themselves other than what was given to them, in turn, by their own parents. All too many Indian Hindu youth, on the other hand, find themselves un-attracted to a religion that is little comprehended or respected by most of those around them – Hindu and non-Hindu alike.

Today's Hindu youth seek more strenuously convincing reasons for following a religion than merely the argument that it is the family tradition. Today's Hindu youth demand, and deserve, cogent philosophical explanations about what the Vedic tradition actually teaches, and why they should remain Vedic rather than join any of the many other religious alternatives that they see around them. Temple priests are often ill equipped to give these bright Hindu youth the answers they so sincerely seek…mom and dad are usually even less knowledgeable than the temple *pujaris*. What is a Hindu child to do?

As I travel the nation delivering lectures on Vedic philosophy and spirituality, I frequently encounter a repeated scenario. Indian Hindu parents will often approach me after I have finished my lecture and timidly ask if they can have some advice. The often-repeated story goes somewhat like this:

> "We raised our son/daughter to be a good Hindu. We took them to the temple for important holidays. We even sent him/her to a Hindu camp for a weekend when they were 13. Now at the age of 23, our child has left the Vedic religion and converted to the (*fill in the blank*) religion. When we ask how could they have left the religion of their family, the answer that they throw back in our face is: 'but mama/dada, you always taught us that all religions are the same, and that it doesn't really matter how a person worships God. So what does it matter if we've followed your advice and switched to another religion? What is so special about Sanatana Dharma if all

religions are equal to it?'"

Many of you currently reading this article have probably been similarly approached by parents expressing this same dilemma. The truly sad thing about this scenario is that the child is, of course, quite correct in her assertion that she is only following the logical conclusion of her parents' often-repeated faux *mantra* of "*all religions are the same.*" If all religions are exactly the same, after all, and if we all just end up in the exact same place in the end anyway, then what does it really matter what religion we follow?

Hindu parents complain when their children adopt other religions, but without understanding that it was precisely this highly flawed dogma of Radical Universalism ("*all religions are the same*"), and not some inherent flaw of Sanatana Dharma itself, that has driven their children away. My contention is that parents themselves are not to be blamed for espousing this anti-Vedic idea to their children. Rather, much of the blame is to be placed at the feet of today's ill equipped Vedic teachers and leaders, the supposed guardians of authentic Dharma teachings.

Failed Leadership in the Vedic Community

Tragically, the vast majority of our present-day, self-proclaimed *gurus*, *swamis*, *yogis*, *mahants*, and Vedic leaders have failed to properly lead the world Vedic community. With a small handful of notable exceptions, the majority of our *gurus* today find themselves quite ill-prepared and unqualified in character, education, doctrinal training, spiritual realization, courage and leadership qualities to be serving in the offices they proclaim for themselves.

Today's failed leaders of the Vedic tradition are not thoroughly educated in either orthodox and traditionalist - i.e., scripturally based - Vedic philosophy, or in the philosophies of such opposing schools of thought (*purva-paksha*) as Judaism, Christianity, Islam, Marxism, Socialism/Communism, Feminism, Left-Hand Path Luciferianism, Anti-Natalism, Buddhism, Darwinian Evolution, Critical Theory, and Scientific Materialism, among many other concocted dogmas spawned in modernity.

They do not have the courage or power of their convictions to present Sanatana Dharma in its gloriously unadulterated and pure form, but wish instead to perpetually water it down out of dread and fear that they may offend one person in their audiences of wealthy Americans - this, even though any American who would come to a talk by an ostensibly Vedic *guru* is obviously there because they have left their old faiths behind, and want to learn about authentic Sanatana Dharma. Rather than delivering what these innocent seekers are yearning for, too many of these self-serving fraudulent "*gurus*" instead give them a falsified version of Sanatana Dharma. They give their innocent audiences - both Indian and non-Indian alike - various degrees of Radical Universalism instead.

The Art of Mountain Climbing

In modern Neo-Hinduism, we hear from a variety of uninformed sources this illogical claim that all religions are equal. Unfortunately, the most damaging source of this fallacy is none other than the many un-informed spiritual leaders of the Hindu community itself. I have been to innumerable *pravachanas* (religious talks), for example, where a benignly grinning, but woefully unknowledgeable, "*guruji*" will provide his gullible audience with the following tediously parroted metaphor, what I call the Mountain Metaphor.

The Mountain Metaphor:

"Truth (or God or Brahman) lies at the summit of a very high mountain. There are many, many diverse paths to reach the top of the mountain, and thus attain the one supreme goal. Some paths are shorter, some longer. The path itself, however, is unimportant. The only truly important thing is that seekers all reach the top of the mountain. All paths reach the top of the mountain."

While this simplistic metaphor might seem compelling at a cursory glance, it leaves out a very important elemental supposition:

It makes the unfounded assumption that everyone wants to get to the top of the same mountain!

As we will soon see, not every religion shares the same goal, the same conception of the Absolute (indeed, even the belief that there is an Absolute), or the same means to their respective, and radically different, goals. Rather than there being only one "mountain", there are actually many different philosophical "mountains", each with their own very unique claim to be the supreme goal of all human spiritual striving. As I will show, Radical Universalism is not only an idea that is riddled with self-contradictory implications, but it is a doctrine that never originated from traditional Sanatana Dharma at all. It is in actuality thoroughly anti-Sanatana Dharma (adharmic) through and through.

Chapter Two: A Tradition of Consideration, Not Capitulation

Historically, pre-colonial classical Sanatana Dharma never taught that all religions are the same. This is not to say, however, that Sanatana Dharma has not believed in respectful consideration for other religions or freedom of religious thought and expression. Sanatana Dharma has very clearly always been a religion that has taught patient forbearance of other generally positive religious traditions.

However, the assertion that a) we should have respectful consideration for the beliefs of other religions is a radically different claim from the overreaching declaration that b) all religions are the same. And this confusion between two thoroughly separate assertions may be one reason why so many modern Hindus believe that the respectful consideration extended to other religions by Sanatana Dharma is synonymous with Radical Universalism. It is not. To maintain a healthy tolerance of another person's religion does not mean that we have to then adopt that person's religion! Tolerance does not mean acceptance.

Traditional Vedic religion has always been the most broadminded, patient and openhearted of all religions in history, bar none. This inherently Vedic broadmindedness and rational acceptance of the differences in others is expressed, for example, in the famous adage from the *Maha Upanishad* (6.73) that states: *vasudhaiva kutumbakam* - "The world is one family." Sanatana Dharma is not a religion that persecutes others merely for having a difference in theological belief.

Vedic India, for example, has been one of the sole nations on Earth where the Christian community was able to live in peace with its neighbors. This is the case despite the presence of Christianity in India for almost 2,000 years. Similarly, Zoroastrian refugees escaping the destruction of the Persian civilization at the hands of Islamic conquerors were greeted with welcome refuge in India over 1,000 years ago. The Zoroastrian community (now known as the Parsee community) in India has thrived in all these many centuries, living together with their Dharmi neighbors in peace and mutual respect.

In keeping with the time-honored Vedic adage that the guest in one's home is to be treated with as much hospitality as one would treat a visiting divinity, Sanatana Dharma has always been gracious to the followers of non-Vedic (*avaidika*) religions, and respectful of the gods, scriptures and customs of others. Sanatana Dharma has been a religion that has always sought to live side-by-side peacefully with the followers of other, non-Vedic, religions, whether they were the indigenous Indian religions of Buddhism, Jainism, and Sikhism, or the foreign religions of Christianity and Islam. The tolerance and openness of Sanatana Dharma has been historically unprecedented among the wider community of world religions, universally acclaimed, and very well attested.

The common error that is often made, however, is to confuse the long-held Vedic tradition of tolerating other religions with the mistaken notion that Sanatana Dharma consequently encourages us to believe that all religions are exactly the same. We have mistaken Vedic tolerance with Radical Universalism. The two are, by far, not the same. The leap from tolerance of other faiths to a belief that all religions are equal is not a leap that is grounded in logic. Nor is it grounded in the history, literature, or philosophy of the Vedic tradition itself.

In general, many of the world's religions have been periodically guilty of fomenting rigid sectarianism and intolerance among their followers. We have witnessed, most especially in the records of the more historically recent and highly aggressive Abrahamic religions, that religion has sometimes been used as a destructive mechanism. It has often been misused to divide people, to conquer others in the name of one's god, and to make artificial and oppressive distinctions between "believers" and "non-believers".

Bending Over Backwards with Tolerance

Being an inherently non-fundamentalist and deeply rational world-view, Sanatana Dharma has naturally always been keen to distinguish its own tolerant approach to spirituality vis-à-vis more sectarian and conflict oriented notions of religion. Indeed, many followers of the modern development of Neo-Hinduism are infamous for bending over backwards to show the world just how non-fanatical and open-minded they are. They will often be so passive in their approach to the point of even denying themselves the very right to unapologetically celebrate our own religious tradition. Such a weak-willed and masochistic mindset has led to a form of pathological self-abnegation in the name of tolerance that is alien to the traditional Vedic outlook.

Unfortunately, in their headlong rush to devolve the Vedic tradition of anything that might seem to even remotely resemble the closed-minded sectarianism often found in other religions, Neo-Hindus often forget the obvious truth that the Vedic religion is itself a systematic and self-contained religious tradition in its own right.

Chapter Three: The Distinctively Unique Vedic Religion

In the same manner that the religions of Christianity, Islam, Jainism, Buddhism or Taoism have their own decidedly unique and specific religious beliefs, metaphysical doctrines, ontological preoccupations, philosophical presuppositions, and claims to spiritual authority, all of which fall within the firmly demarcated theological bounds of their own unique traditions, Sanatana Dharma too has just such uniquely Veda-centric theological and institutional bounds.

Like every other religion in the world and throughout history, Sanatana Dharma is a distinct and unique tradition, with its own inbuilt and non-replicable beliefs, world-view, traditions, rituals, concept of the Absolute, metaphysics, ethics, aesthetics, cosmology, cosmogony, and theology.[5] The grand, systematic philosophical construct that we call Sanatana Dharma is the result of the extraordinary revelatory gifts of the great *rishis*, *yogis*, *acharyas*, and *gurus* attested to throughout the history of our religion, guided by the transcendent light of the Vedic revelation, which have stood the test of time. It is a tradition that is worthy of healthy celebration by Dharmis and of deeply respectful admiration by non-Dharmis. We have, in Sanatana Dharma, the preeminent spiritual tradition on Earth that should fill us with a healthy, yet humble, sense of pride.

Followers of Sanatana Dharma have no more reason to be uncomfortable with the singular uniqueness of our own spiritual tradition, and even less of a reason to not boldly assert our own

---

[5] Indeed, for that matter, Sanatana Dharma has its own very unique forms of such "secular" fields as economic theory, political science, sociological sciences, and the sciences in general.

exceptional contributions to the development of global religious thought, than do the followers of any other venerable faith. Indeed, given the fact that Sanatana Dharma is the very first, most ancient, most comprehensively reasonable and most philosophically incomparable of all religions on Earth, we have even more reason to deeply revere our religious tradition.

This is an obvious, yet all too often forgotten, fact the importance of which cannot be overstated: *Sanatana Dharma is its own uniquely independent religious tradition, different and distinct from any other religion on Earth.* There is a unique and incomparable Vedic philosophy, a Vedic world-view; a Vedic set of ethics; a Vedic theology; a Vedic spiritual and temporal culture; a Vedic view on the nature of God (Ishvara), personhood (*jiva*) and material reality (*jagat*), all of which are completely distinct from those of any other religion on Earth. In short, there is a distinctly Vedic tradition that has zero dependence upon or appropriation from any other religious tradition for its own spiritual wealth.

Such a justifiable recognition of Sanatana Dharma's unique features is not to deny that there will always be several important similarities between many of the religions of the world. Indeed, the human impetus to know Truth being a universally experienced phenomenon, it would be quite surprising indeed if there were not some common features discernable among all the diverse religions of our common earth. Similarity, however, is not sameness.

While a few interesting commonalities and similarities can always be seen and appreciated, it would be misleading to consequently deny that Sanatana Dharma, like every other separate religious tradition, is also to be plainly contrasted in myriad ways from any other religion. Indeed, there are arguably an infinitely larger number of differences between Sanatana Dharma and other religions than there are similarities. Such a realization and acceptance of Sanatana Dharma's unique place in the world does not, by any stretch of the imagination, have to lead automatically to sectarianism, strife, conflict, or religious chauvinism – as some radical secularists and weak-hearted modern Neo-Hindus dishonestly wish to contend.

Indeed, such a recognition of Sanatana Dharma's distinctiveness is crucial if Dharmis are to possess even a modicum of healthy self-understanding, self-respect, and pride in their own tradition. Self-respect and the ability to celebrate one's unique spiritual tradition are basic psychological needs, and a cherished civil right of any human being, Vedic and non-Vedic alike.

Chapter Four: Letting the Tradition Speak for Itself

When we look at the philosophical, literary, and historical sources of the pre-colonial Vedic tradition, we find that the notion of Radical Universalism is overwhelmingly absent. The idea that *"all religions are the same"* is not found anywhere in the sacred literature of Sanatana Dharma, anywhere among the utterances of the great philosopher-*acharyas* of Sanatana Dharma, or in any of Sanatana Dharma's six main schools of philosophical thought (the *Shad-darshanas*). Throughout the history of the tradition, such great Vedic philosophers as Narada, Shandilya, Yajnavalkya, Vyasa, Bodhayana, Patanjali, Shankara, Ramanuja, Madhva, Vallabha, Chaitanya, Vijnana Bhikshu, Swami Narayana (Sahajananda Swami), and many thousands of other similar Vedic sages made very unambiguous and unapologetic distinctions between the religion of Sanatana

Dharma and non-Vedic religions.

The sages of pre-modern Sanatana Dharma had no difficulty in boldly asserting what was, and what was not, to be considered Vedic. And they did so extremely often! This lucid sense of religious community and philosophical clarity is seen first and foremost in the very question of what, precisely, constitutes a follower of Sanatana Dharma. Without knowing the answer to this most foundational of questions, it is impossible to fully assess the damaging inadequacies of Radical Universalist dogma.

Who is a Dharmi?

Remarkably, when the question of who is a Dharmi is discussed today, specifically among many Neo-Hindus, but among many outside of our religion as well, we get a multitude of confused, contrived and contradictory answers from both Vedic laypersons and from most supposed Vedic leaders. The very fact that we have such a difficult time in understanding the simple answer to even so fundamental a question as "who is a Dharmi?" is a starkly sad indicator of the lack of knowledge in the Neo-Hindu community today.

Some of the more simplistically infantile and incorrect answers to this question include:

a) Anyone who has been born in India is automatically a Dharmi (the natal fallacy).
b) If your parents are Dharmis, then you are a Dharmi (the familial argument).
c) If you are born into a certain caste, then you are a Dharmi (the genetic inheritance fallacy).
d) If you believe in *karma* and reincarnation, then you are Dharmi (forgetting that many non-Vedic religions share at least some of

the beliefs of Sanatana Dharma).

e) If you practice any religion originating from India (Jainism, Buddhism or Sikhism), then you are a Dharmi (the national origin fallacy).

None of the above answers to the question "who is a Dharmi?" is correct. The real answer to this question has already been conclusively answered by the ancient sages of Sanatana Dharma, and is actually much simpler to ascertain than we would guess.

The two primary identifying factors that distinguish the individual uniqueness of each of the larger world religious traditions are a) the scriptural authority upon which the tradition is based, and b) the fundamental religious tenet(s) that it espouses and that its followers are expected to adhere to. If we ask the question "what is a follower of the religion of Judaism?", for example, the accepted answer is: someone who accepts the Torah as their scriptural guide and believes in the monotheistic concept of God espoused in those scriptures. "What is a Christian?": a person who accepts the Gospels and the New Testament as their scriptural guide and believes that Jesus is the incarnate God who died for their sins. "What is a Muslim?": someone who accepts the Qur'an as their scriptural guide, and believes that there is no God but Allah, and that Mohammed is his prophet. We can continue in the same vein for all of the other larger religions in our world today.

In general, what determines whether a person is a follower of any particular religion is the simple criterion of whether or not they accept, and attempt to live by, the scriptural authority of that religion. This criterion is no less true of Sanatana Dharma than it is of any other religion upon the face of the Earth today. Thus, the question of "who is a Dharmi?" is similarly very easily answered. By definition, a Dharmi - a follower of the Vedic tradition - is an individual who accepts as authoritatively valid the religious guidance of the Vedic scriptures, and who strives to live in accordance with Dharma, God's divine laws as revealed in the Vedic scriptures. What it means to be a **Vedic person** is that, by very definition, you accept the authority of the *Vedas*!

In keeping with this standard definition, all of the Dharmi thinkers of the six traditional schools of Vedic philosophy (the *shad-darshanas*) insisted on the acceptance of the scriptural authority (*shabda-pramana*) of the *Vedas* as the primary criterion for distinguishing a follower of Sanatana Dharma from a non-Vedic person, as well as distinguishing overtly Vedic philosophical positions from non-Vedic ones. It has been the historically accepted standard that, if you accept the *Vedas* (meaning the complete *shruti* and *smrti* canon of the Vedic scriptures, such as the four *Vedas, Brahmanas,*

Aranyakas, Upanishads, Mahabharata, Ramayana, Bhagavad Gita, Puranas, Dharma Shastras, etc.) as your ultimate scriptural authority, and if you live your life in accordance with the Dharmic principles of the *Vedas*, you are then a full-fledged and fully accepted Dharmi. Thus, the only authentic and accepted criteria for whether a person is or is not a follower of Sanatana Dharma are, respectively, the following:

> Acceptance of *Vedas* = Dharmi
>
> Rejection of *Vedas* = non-Dharmi

Sanatana Dharma is Not Synonymous with Being Indian

The above criterion is the sole criterion determining whether or not a person is a follower of Sanatana Dharma, and not the individual's ethnicity, or nation of origin, or any other telluric factor. Thus, any South Asian Indian who rejects the authority of the *Vedas* is obviously not a Dharmi, and that is true regardless of their birth. While, on the other hand, an American, Canadian, German, Russian, Spaniard, Italian, British, Croatian, Lithuanian, Brazilian, Chilean, Costa Rican, Indonesian, Cambodian, Thai, Australian, Afrikaner, or Indian who does accept the authority of the *Vedas* as their supreme spiritual guide, and who seriously follows the practices of Sanatana Dharma in his daily life, obviously is a Dharmi. One is a Dharmi, not by the clout of his ethnicity, but by acceptance of the Vedic scriptures and by the practice of Dharma.

Chapter Five: Clearly Defining Sanatana Dharma

To state that the Vedic tradition is the most ancient continuously practiced religious tradition on the face of the earth is a tremendous understatement of this fact. In actuality, Sanatana Dharma has existed previous to the creation of our very universe itself. Sanatana Dharma is an eternal spiritual phenomenon the origin of which is God Himself. Being an eternal phenomenon, the origin and nature of which transcends the material world, the essential principles of Sanatana Dharma do not change, ever. They are unalterable and immutable.

This fact being the case, the principles of Sanatana Dharma are just as applicable and true in the 21st century as they were 10,000 years ago. It is those who understand and fully embrace the non-alterable nature of Sanatana Dharma who can be justifiably termed followers of authentic Sanatana Dharma. Authentic Sanatana Dharma is predicated upon many unalterable and axiomatic principles, the foundation of which are the unalterable epistemological principles (*pramanas*) of Vedic philosophy. These epistemological principles are agreed upon and accepted by every single ancient[6] *rishi*, *guru*, Acharya and *pandita* in the Vedic tradition. The most important of the epistemological principles of Sanatana Dharma are the following:

1. The Vedic Scriptures

All spiritual knowledge is based upon Vedic *Shastra* (scriptures) alone.[7] If there is any spiritual or philosophical pronouncement that cannot be

---

[6] In this case, "ancient" indicating every single legitimate Vedic *rishi*, *guru*, Acharya and *pandita* previous to the era of Modernity, i.e., previous to the last roughly 200-300 years.
[7] In this regard, the *Brahma Sutras* (1.1.3) state *shastra-yonitvat*, "The Vedic scriptures are the means of knowing God."

supported by the supreme and eternal authority of the Vedic scriptures, then authentic Sanatana Dharma makes it clear that such a pronouncement is to be utterly rejected as necessarily untrue.

2. Pramana

Sanatana Dharma accepts a limited number of foundational *pramanas*, or valid means of cognition,[8] for determining the validity of any truth-claim. If any truth-claim, either factual (*apara*) or spiritual (*para*) in nature, cannot be demonstrated via its ontologically corresponding *pramana*, then that truth-claim is rejected as having been conclusively disproven.

---

[8] Also known as proper epistemic mechanisms.

These *pramanas* are:

   A) *Pratyaksha* – Empirically derived data.

   B) *Anumana* – Inferential knowledge derived via logic, mathematical principles, etc.

   C) *Shabda* – Knowledge that is derived from purely transcendental and divine sources.[9].

   D) *Rishi-Upadesha* – The teachings of the Rishis (revealers of the Vedic scriptures).

This last foundational epistemological principle of authentic Sanatana Dharma consists of the instructions (*upadesha*) of recognized *rishis* (seers and revealers of the Vedic scriptures), legitimate *gurus*

---

[9] *Shabda* is thus the sonic basis of the literary instantiation of *Shastra*.

and authorized *Acharyas* (Preceptors representing a traditional and scripturally recognized Vedic tradition).

The highest Truths of Vedic knowledge are not revealed by prophets, as in the Abrahamic tradition. Nor is Truth revealed by the speculative or experimental methods of materialistic science. Rather, Truth is revealed in the Vedic tradition via those perfected beings who have directly experienced Truth first-hand on the very plane of Transcendence itself via meditation and the spiritual purification of their beings by *sadhana* (systematic spiritual practice). These epistemological principles are only a few of the many elements that make Sanatana Dharma unique and unlike any other religious or spiritual path that exists in this world.

Tragically, the modernist-inspired fad of Neo-Hinduism thoroughly rejects these epistemological principles of authentic Sanatana Dharma in favor of diversity, inclusiveness and equity of all religions. In so doing, it rejects the philosophical heritage of the Vedic tradition entirely.

Traditional Vedic philosophers continually emphasized the crucial importance of clearly understanding the distinction of what was Vedic proper versus what were non-Vedic religious paths. You cannot claim to be a Dharmi, after all, if you do not even understand what it is that you claim to believe, and what it is that others believe.

One set of antonymous Sanskrit terms repeatedly employed by many traditional Vedic philosophers were the words *vaidika* and *avaidika*.[10] The word *vaidika* (or "Vedic" in English) means one who fully

---

[10] The dual terms *vaidika* / *avaidika* stand in a disjunctive relationship with one another. They are an either-or proposition. One is either *vaidika*, or one is *avaidika*. **VvA**. One cannot logically be both simultaneously.

accepts the teachings of the *Vedas*. It refers specifically to the unique epistemological stance taken by the traditional schools of Vedic philosophy, known as *shabda-pramana*, or employing the divine sound current of the *Vedas* as a means of acquiring valid knowledge. In this sense, the word "*vaidika*" is traditionally employed to differentiate those schools of philosophy found within the South Asian context that accept the epistemological validity of the *Vedas* as *apaurusheya*, or a perfect authoritative spiritual source, eternal and untouched by the speculations of humanity, juxtaposed with the *avaidika* schools that do not ascribe such validity to the *Vedas*.

In pre-Christian times, *avaidika* schools were clearly identified by Vedic authors as being specifically the ideologies of Buddhism, Jainism, and the atheistic Charvaka school, all of whom did not accept the *Vedas*. These three schools were unanimously recognized, both by traditional Vedic scholars and by traditional non-Vedic scholars who represented these three schools, as philosophical world-views that rejected the *Vedas*, and which were thus, by definition, non-Vedic. They certainly are to be recognized as being geographically "**Indian**" religions, but they are not theologically/philosophically **Vedic** religions.

Manu, one of the great ancient law-givers of the Vedic tradition, states the following in his *Manava-dharma-shastra*:

> "All those traditions and all those disreputable systems of philosophy that are not based on the *Veda* produce no positive result after death; for they are declared to be founded on darkness. All those doctrines differing from the *Veda* that spring up and soon perish are ineffectual and misleading, because they are of modern date."
>
> (*Manava Dharma Shastra*, 12.95)

Stated in simpler terms, "*vaidika*" specifically refers to those persons who accept the *Vedas* as their sacred scripture, and thus as their source of valid knowledge about spiritual matters. Thus, again, if one does not accept the perfect authority of the *Vedas*, then one is not a follower of Sanatana Dharma in any way, shape or form.[11]

In his famous compendium of all the known South Asian schools of philosophy,[12] the *Sarva-darshana-samgraha,* Madhava Acharya (a 14th century Advaita philosopher; not to be confused with the Vaishnava Madhva who founded Dvaita Vedanta in the 13th century) unambiguously states that Charvakins (atheist empiricists), "Bauddhas" (Buddhists) and "Arhatas" (Jains) are among the non-Vedic, and

---

[11] By extension, it would be wholly justifiable to state that if one does not fully accept the perfect authority of the *Vedas*, then they cannot consider themselves to be a "Hindu" in any true and meaningful sense.

[12] Including both *vaidika* and *avaidika* schools.

thus illegitimate, schools of thought. Conversely, he lists Paniniya, Vaishnava, Shaiva and others among the Vedic, or legitimate, traditions. Very simply, the illegitimate schools are classified as such because they reject the *Vedas*, whereas the legitimate schools accept the *Vedas*.

Likewise, in his *Prasthanabheda*, the well-known Madhusudana Sarasvati (fl. 17th century C.E.) compares and contrasts all the *mleccha* (or "barbaric") viewpoints with Vedic views, and says that the former are not even worthy of consideration, whereas the Buddhist views must at least be considered and debated. We know from an examination of the Vedic scriptures that Buddhism, at least, must be taken slightly more seriously as a philosophical system because Gautama Buddha himself is understood to be an *avesha-avatara* of the Supreme Godhead of Sanatana Dharma, Sriman Narayana.

The differentiation between orthodox and heterodox religion, from a classical Vedic perspective, rests upon acceptance of the Vedic revelation, with the latter rejecting the sanctity of the *Vedas*. As a further attempt to clearly distinguish between Vedic and non-Vedic, the traditional philosophers of Sanatana Dharma regularly used the Sanskrit disjunctive terms *astika* and *nastika* in their writings. These two technical terms are synonymous with *vaidika* and *avaidika*, respectively. *Astika* refers to those who believe in the *Vedas*, *nastika* to those who reject the *Vedas*.

Under the *astika* category, Sanatana Dharma would include any Vedic path that accepts the *Vedas*, such as Vaishnavism, Shaivism, Shaktism, Advaita, Sankhya, Yoga, Nyaya, Mimamsa, among others. The *nastika* religions would include any religious tradition that does not accept the *Vedas*, such as: Buddhism, Jainism, Sikhism, Judaism, Christianity,

Islam, Baha'i, etc.[13] Thus when it came to the importance of unambiguously differentiating between the original and pristine teachings of Sanatana Dharma, versus the teachings of non-Vedic religions, the most historically important sages of Vedic philosophical and theological thought all spoke with one clear voice as advocates of Vaidika Dharma - Sanatana Dharma - as a systematic, unitive tradition of spiritual expression based upon the unique and unequaled Vedic revelation.

---

[13] Additionally, in the 21st century, we would also include under the labels of avaidika/nastika such contemporary ideologies as Marxism, Social Darwinism, Liberalism, Capitalism, Feminism, Left-Hand Path, Luciferianism, Anti-Natalism and every form of Atheism.

Chapter Six: Dharma Rakshakas – The Defenders of Dharma

With the stark exception of very recent times, Sanatana Dharma has historically always been recognized as a separate and distinct religious phenomenon, as a tradition unto itself, in comparison to every other, more recent, religion in the world. It was recognized as a unique tradition by both outside observers of Sanatana Dharma, as well as from within, by Sanatana Dharma's greatest spiritual teachers. The philosophers, saints and sages of Sanatana Dharma continuously strived to uphold the sanctity and gift of the Vedic worldview, often under the barrages of direct polemic opposition by non-Vedic traditions. Sanatana Dharma, Buddhism, Jainism, and Charvaka (atheists), the four main philosophical schools found in South Asian history, would frequently engage each other in painstakingly precise debates, arguing compellingly over even the smallest conceptual minutia of philosophical subject matter.

In the 20th century, this ancient routine of critiquing and defeating *purva-paksha* (opposing) philosophical world-views from the Vedic perspective continues unabated in the form of my philosophical critiques of many modern ideologies, as well as the many educational projects of the International Sanatana Dharma Society. But rather than merely limiting ourselves to critiquing the world-views of more ancient schools of thought, in our ongoing campaign to uphold the philosophical preeminence of Sanatana Dharma, we are now necessarily engaged in polemic encounters with the many ideologies that have sprouted up within the context of modernity. Thus, we now find ourselves engaged in successful disputations with such anti-Vedic ideologies as Abrahamism, Marxism, Socialism, Feminism, Globalism, Transhumanism, Transgenderism, anti-Natalism, New Age ideas, and Left-Hand Path/Luciferianism, among others.

Whether referring to Vedic refutation of non-Vedic world-views in antiquity, or such refutations performed up to this very moment, authentic Sanatana Dharma has always defended itself vigorously from any anti-Vedic opposition.

The sapient sages of Sanatana Dharma have always met such philosophical challenges with cogent argumentation, rigid logic, and sustained pride in their tradition, always soundly defeating their philosophical opponents in open debate. In almost any debate involving knowledgeable and well-trained representatives of Sanatana Dharma versus the representatives of non-Vedic schools of thought, the Vedic philosopher would invariably win the debate hands down.

Shankara Acharya, as only one of a vast multiplicity of examples of Vedic *acharyas* courageously defending their religion, earned the title "Digvijaya", or "Conqueror of all Directions". This indomitable title was awarded to Shankara due solely to his formidable ability to defend the Vedic tradition from the philosophical incursions of opposing (*purva-paksha*), non-Vedic schools of thought. Indeed, Shankara is universally attributed by both scholars, as well as later, post-Shankaran Vedic leaders, with being partially responsible for the historical decline of Buddhism in India due to his intensely polemic missionary activities.

Shankaracharya traversed the length and breadth of India defeating Buddhist and other non-Vedic philosophers, and showing conclusively and unapologetically the superiority of thought of the Vedic tradition. No Radical Universalist was he!

The great Vaishnava teacher, philosopher and *bhakta* (devotee) Ramanuja Acharya traversed India engaging in debates with Buddhists and Jains and is known to have converted many thousands of them to Sanatana Dharma.[14] The Acharya Madhva is similarly seen as being responsible for the sharp decline of Jainism in South India due to his immense debating skills in defense of Sanatana Dharma. Madhva is known to have converted thousands of Buddhist and Jain leaders to the light of Vedic spirituality. Chaitanya Mahaprabhu has been documented in the texts *Chaitanya Charitamrita* and *Chaitanya Bhagavata* as likewise converting many Muslims, Buddhists, Jains, and atheists to Sanatana Dharma in the early 16th century.

All pre-modern Vedic sages, Acharyas and philosophers recognized and celebrated the singularly unique vision that Sanatana Dharma had to offer the world, clearly distinguished between

---

[14] This was especially the case in the Mysore and Deccan areas of India. One famous person, as only one example, who Ramanuja Acharya converted from Jainism to Sanatana Dharma was King Bitti Deva of the Hoysala kingdom, who consequently changed his name to the Vedic name Vishnuvardhana.

Vedic and non-Vedic religions, and defended the distinctiveness and exceptionality of Sanatana Dharma to the utmost of their formidable intellectual and spiritual abilities. They did so unapologetically, professionally, and courageously as our great Dharma Rakshakas – or Defenders of Dharma. None of our ancient and authentic *rishis*, *gurus* and Acharyas viewed Sanatana Dharma to be in any way the same, equal to, or interchangeable with other non-Vedic religions. None of them considered all religions to be the same. The Vedic world-view only makes sense, has value, and has a hope of surviving into the future if, and only if, we all similarly celebrate its irreplaceable uniqueness today.

Chapter Seven: Traditional Sanatana Dharma Versus Modern Neo-Hinduism

A disastrous detour in the very long history of Sanatana Dharma was witnessed throughout the 19th century, the destructive magnitude of which only a very few Vedic leaders and scholars today are barely beginning to adequately assess and address. This very modern development both altered and weakened the ancient tradition of Sanatana Dharma to such a tremendous degree that Sanatana Dharma has only just begun to recover from the damage.

The classical, traditional Sanatana Dharma that had been responsible for the continuous existence of an exceedingly sophisticated degree of culture, architecture, music, philosophy, ritual, and theology over many thousands of years came under devastating intellectual and psychological assault during the 19th century British colonial rule like at no other time in the Vedic religion's history.

For a thousand years previous to the British Raj, brutal Islamic marauders had repeatedly attempted to destroy Sanatana Dharma through overt physical genocide of multiple tens of millions of followers of Sanatana Dharma, as well as the systematic destruction of many tens of thousands of Vedic temples, the burning of multiple libraries containing vast numbers of books and manuscripts constituting the ancient literary heritage of Vedic arts and sciences, the dismantling of many Vedic institutes of learning, and the destroying of multiple sacred places.

In their clumsy and ignorance-fueled barbarism, Islam tried to physically annihilate everything and anything Vedic. The end result of their attempt to eradicate Dharma produced the first, and arguably largest, instances of physical genocide of a people seen throughout the annals of human history. The multiple Vedic peoples, ranging from parts of Iran to as far east as Indonesia, experienced a devastating holocaust like no other people have ever experienced in all of human history. Today, barely four-hundred years after the British put an end to the Islamic genocide, Sanatana Dharma has only begun its recovery process in full.

Traditional Sanatana Dharma's wise sages and noble warriors had fought bravely over the course of several hundred years to stem this anti-Vedic holocaust to the best of their ability, more often than not paying for their bravery with the forfeiture of their lives. The total physical annihilation of Vedic culture was arguably prevented only by the arrival of the British and their eventual subjugation of the Vedic people to the global dominion of the British Empire. What the Vedic community consequently experienced under British

Christian/Free Masonic domination, however, was an ominously innovative form of cultural genocide that, while not as brutishly physical as the Islamic attempts to wipe out Vedic culture, was just as destructive to the collective psyche of the Vedic people.

What the traditional Vedic peoples endured under the British Raj was not an attempt at the physical annihilation of their religion, but a deceivingly more subtle program of intellectual and spiritual subversion designed to warp traditional Vedic spirituality from within its own supposed ranks. It is easy for a people to understand the urgent existential threat posed by a barbarous enemy that seeks to literally kill them. It is much harder, though, to fully comprehend the threat of an enemy who, while remaining just as deadly in their intentions, claims to seek only to serve a subjugated people's best interests. The British Raj posed just as much of an existential threat to traditional Vedic culture as did the Islamic conqueror. But the British were intelligent enough to employ native "Hindus" to do their dirty work, rather than make their attacks against Sanatana Dharma overtly obvious.

During this short span of time in the 19th century, the ancient grandeur and beauty of a classical Sanatana Dharma that had stood the test of thousands of years, came under direct ideological attack. What makes this period in Vedic history most especially tragic is that the main apparatus that the British used in their attempts to destroy traditional Sanatana Dharma were the British educated, spiritually co-opted sons and daughters of Sanatana Dharma herself. Seeing traditional Sanatana Dharma through the eyes of their British globalist masters, a pandemic wave of 19th century Anglicized "Hindu" intellectuals[15] saw it as their

---

[15] This class of Anglicized-Indian urban pseudo-intellectuals came to be known as the Bhadralok class among their fellow Bengalis.

solemn duty to "Westernize" and "modernize" traditional Sanatana Dharma in order to make it more palatable to their new European globalist overlords.

One of the phenomena that occurred during this historic period was the fabrication of a new movement now known as "Neo-Hinduism". Neo-Hinduism was an artificial religious construct used as a paradigmatic juxtaposition to the legitimate and traditional Sanatana Dharma that had been the religion and culture of the people for thousands of years previously. Neo-Hinduism was used as an effective weapon to replace authentic Sanatana Dharma with a British invented and encouraged imitation of Vedic religion now rechristened "Hinduism". Neo-Hinduism was, in actuality, the newly triumphant world-view of Abrahamist-Masonic Modernity with an Indian face. This new religious movement was designed to make a subjugated people easier to manage and control.

The new phenomenon of Neo-Hinduism was radically distinct from the traditional and authentic religion of Sanatana Dharma that had preceded it. Rather, it was something brand new and designedly subversive. Neo-Hinduism was a wholly different and concocted trojan horse manufactured by India's new colonial overlords to destroy the remnants of Vedic civilization from within. In the historically unprecedented interface between Vedic civilization and the newly emerged project of globalist modernity that occurred in the very early 19th century, authentic Sanatana Dharma looked at the world-view of modernity, critiqued it and then rejected it. Neo-Hinduism, on the other hand, unthinkingly and unashamedly capitulated to modernity. Neo-Hinduism represents the full-blown surrender of modernist trained, 19th century "Hindu" intellectuals to Abrahamist-Masonic Modernity.

The Christian and British Masonic inspired neo-Hinduism movement attempted to execute several overlapping goals, and did so with unfortunate success. These goals include the following:

> a) The subtle Christianization of Vedic theology, which included concerted and vicious attacks on iconic imagery (*archana*, or *murti*); rejection of the epistemic legitimacy of the *Shruti* portion of the Vedic scriptures; the undermining of Vedic panentheism;[16] and the ridiculing of the Vedic people's continued belief in the beloved gods and goddesses of traditional Sanatana Dharma.
>
> b) The imposition of the highly limited and flawed Western scientific method,

---

[16] Panentheism is the Vedic teaching that God is both wholly transcendent vis-à-vis the material world, while simultaneously interpenetrating all of reality as its sustaining foundation. God is both fully transcendent and fully immanent.

"rationalism", and nihilistic skepticism on the study of Sanatana Dharma in order to demonstrate Sanatana Dharma's supposedly inferior grasp of reality and methodology.

c) Ongoing attacks against the ancient Vedic science of ritual in the name of simplification and democratization of worship.

d) Convincing followers of Sanatana Dharma that the overtly Christian doctrine of "turning the other cheek" was somehow actually a Vedic doctrine, with the consequent emasculation of the Vedic mass psyche.[17]

---

[17] This specific goal has been greatly expanded in the 21st century to now include the forcefully prescribed acceptance of the postmodern "LGBTQ", feminist and transexual phenomena in a concerted attempt to transform Sanatana Dharma from the strong, Dharma-warrior culture that was traditionally one of its chief foundations, to a more cosmopolitan and effeminate caricature that is designed to weaken the Vedic family to the maximal degree.

e) The importation of Radical Universalism from liberal and globalist oriented Unitarian/Universalist Christianity as a device designed to severely water down traditional Vedic philosophy.

The world-view of Neo-Hinduism is, in almost every single aspect of its ideology, thoroughly opposed to the philosophical foundations of authentic Sanatana Dharma. The dogmas outlined in the following chapter are only a small number of major features that are at the heart of Neo-Hindu ideology and practice.

Chapter Eight: The Dogmas of Neo-Hinduism

Almost every single foundational dogma of the Neo-Hindu movement stands in direct opposition to the views of Sanatana Dharma. These are several dogmas of Neo-Hinduism, along with explanations of why they are non-Vedic beliefs.

1) Self-Abnegating Hyper-Tolerance

Sanatana Dharma has historically always been a world-view that has encouraged reasoned open-mindedness and rational tolerance of other, non-Vedic world-views. Sanatana Dharma has never believed or engaged in the persecution of ethically-based ideologies, even if they stood apart from the Vedic tradition. The new cult of Neo-Hinduism, however, since its inception, has encouraged a non-rational and pathological form of hyper "tolerance" that knows no rational limits within the normative and accepted bounds of the self-preservation of Sanatana Dharma itself.

In its puerile attempts to bow down to the sentiments and demands of every other religion in the world, Neo-Hinduism has very often callously sacrificed the unique identity of Sanatana Dharma itself upon the altar of ecumenism, "interfaith dialogue" and globalism. Neo-Hindus have demonstrated an eagerly hair-triggered meekness, cowardice, debilitating shyness and embarrassingly apologetic attitude vis-à-vis all other non-Vedic religions to the clear point of self-flagellating religio-masochism. Rational tolerance is often a positive virtue to exhibit toward "the other"; but not to the point of the thorough abnegation of one's very self in the process. Sanatana Dharma does not teach us to commit religious suicide in the name of tolerance. It teaches us to have a strong and healthy sense of pride in our ancient tradition.

2) "Reforming" the Perfect

Neo-Hinduism is not an ideology that was born from the Vedic tradition. Rather, it is entirely sourced in the Abrahamist/Modernist geopolitical concerns of the 19th century British Empire, and is thus completely alien to the Vedic tradition. Neo-Hinduism is a Trojan horse modelled ideology that was designed to subvert Sanatana Dharma from within with the aim of reconstituting the Vedic tradition in wholly Abrahamist/Modernist terms. This ongoing project of subversion being the case, another common feature of all Neo-Hindus (both historically and to this very day) is the constant theme that the Vedic tradition is a barbaric and antiquated culture that can only be saved within the context of Modernity by "reforming" it; i.e., by remaking it in the countenance of everything that is "progressive", that is "modern", that is "scientific", that is "Christian", and that is anti-Vedic.

In speaking of the "evils" of traditional India and Sanatana Dharma, Keshub Chandra Sen, one of the most notorious anti-Vedic leaders of the new Neo-Hinduism movement stated that:

> "All the evils which had accumulated in this country in the course of ages at once succumbed to the advancing effects of civilization, and the violent onslaughts, directed by Western education and refinement, naturally tended to destroy all that was wrong and demoralising in this country. So we see, one after the other, the moral, social, and intellectual evils in India gradually fading away. The work is still going on — I mean the work of destruction." (*Keshub Chunder Sen's Lectures in India*, pg. 37)

Repeatedly, ad nauseum, we read in the screeds of the founders and current apologists of Neo-Hinduism endless accusatory tirades against the imaginary "sexism", "class oppression", "social backwardness", and "idol worshipping" of traditional Sanatana Dharma. Thus making the founders of Neo-Hinduism sound more akin to Christian Marxists[18] than anything remotely Vedic.

Not surprisingly, as we will see later in this book, such crypto Christian Marxists in the guise of "Hindus" also offer the same supposed remedies for these social problems as did their liberal globalist overlords: a radical "reform" of the Vedic tradition that will ultimately empty it of anything remotely or authentically Vedic, and a corresponding re-imagining of the Vedic tradition in anti-Vedic terms. Indeed, with the dogma of Radical Universalism as its ideological foundation, the new cult of Neo-Hinduism seeks the thorough eradication of traditional Sanatana Dharma

---

[18] For those unfamiliar with this political phenomenon, there is a religious school of thought termed "Liberation Theology" which has attempted to blend a highly liberal form of Christian theology with the political theories of Marxism. This grotesque theo-political hybrid has been supported by such Catholic theologians as Frei Betto, Gustavo Gutiérrez, Leonardo Boff, Juan Luis Segundo and Jon Sobrino, and is now the unofficial theological position of the Roman Catholic Church as a whole.

altogether – and all in the name of progressivism, globalism, liberalism, mainstream science and all that which is deemed modern.

3) Radical Universalism

It is with the eradication of traditional Sanatana Dharma in mind that Neo-Hinduism has made as its prevailing refrain and its very ideological foundation the globalist claim that *"all religions are the same"*. The aberrant theory of Radical Universalism serves as the very heart of the Neo-Hindu project of subversion of authentic Sanatana Dharma, thus necessitating the creation of this book.

4) Acceptance of All Religions' Scriptures as Equally Valid

The sacred scriptures of Sanatana Dharma are

termed *Shastra* in the perfected Sanskrit language. *Shastra* is a strict technical term that refers exclusively to that specific sacred revelatory literature known as the *Veda*.[19] The position of Sanatana Dharma is that we can know the highest of Truths via the Vedic scripture alone, which is the eternal (*nitya*), non-manmade (*apaurusheya*), and unalterable (*anirvatin*) Truth in literary form. Any other literature that is not recognized as being of the nature of *Shastra* (i.e., Vedic) is not accepted by Sanatana Dharma as having any legitimacy whatsoever. Thus, the Bible, the Qur'an, the Tripitaka, the *Guru Granth Sahib*, the Book of Mormon, or any other non-Vedic literary work, is not accepted as a legitimate scriptural work in the tradition of Sanatana Dharma.

---

[19] The term *Veda* (literally "Knowledge") is a comprehensive phrase that is traditionally understood to mean the totality of both the *Shruti* and *Smriti* literatures. Thus, the *Veda-Samhitas*, *Brahmanas*, *Aranyakas*, *Upanishads*, *Itihasas*, *Puranas*, *Dharma Shastras*, *Sutras*, etc. are all included under the title *Veda*.

Followers of Neo-Hinduism, on the other hand, make the uneducated claim that any "scripture" of any religion, and of all religions, in the world is to be accepted equally as *Shastra*. They equate all other religious writings, even if such a work is no more than two hundred years old, and regardless of the actual theological/philosophical content of that work, as being of equal value in every way to the Vedic scriptures. In making this short-sighted and immensely anti-Vedic assertion, Neo-Hindus have rendered themselves at odds with the emphatic statements of the Vedic scriptures themselves, and have thus implicitly rejected the Vedic religion itself.

5) Panentheistic Monotheism Versus Kathenotheism

Sanatana Dharma is both a rigorously formulated philosophical system and an unalterable theological revelation. On the question of Divine Ontology,

Sanatana Dharma upholds the theological principle of Panentheistic Monotheism; i.e., that there is one ultimate, perfect and supreme Absolute who is both fully transcendent to material reality, while being simultaneously present within all material reality as the source and sustainer of all things, both perceptual and conceptual.

While there is ultimately one, and necessarily only one, supreme God in Sanatana Dharma, there also exists a multitude of lesser divine beings known as *devas* and *devis* (gods and goddesses, respectively), who are thoroughly dependent upon, and servants of, the one supreme God. The *devas* and *devis* occupy an ontological realm of being that is above that of the human (*manushya*), but infinitely below that of God. To use a very imperfect analogy, the *devas* and *devis* are somewhat similar to the Abrahamic concept of angels, who are clearly servants of the Supreme, and not to ever be confused with God Himself.

God[20] is never to be mistaken with His servants, regardless of how powerful or virtuous said servants may be. Lord Sri Krishna in His *Bhagavad Gita* makes it abundantly clear that He is infinitely above the *devas* and *devis*.

"Men of small intelligence worship the demigods, and their fruits are limited and temporary. Those who worship the demigods go to the planets of the demigods, but My devotees ultimately reach My supreme planet." (*Bhagavad Gita*, 7.23)

Despite the fact that almost every Neo-Hindu "teacher" will claim adherence to the *Bhagavad Gita* as the source of their speculative theories, Neo-Hinduism thoroughly rejects Lord Krishna's very clear teachings in the *Bhagavad Gita* on the vast ontological distinction between God (*Vishnu-tattva*)

---

[20] Variously termed 'Brahman', 'Sriman-Narayana', 'Bhagavan', 'Ishvara', 'Purushottama', 'Vishnu', 'Krishna', etc. throughout the Vedic scriptures in accordance with that particular aspect of divine ontology that the specific scripture passage in question is revealing information about.

versus the *devas* and *devis* (*jiva-tattva*).

Rather than grasping the sophisticated concept of Panentheistic Monotheism that is at the heart of all Vedic theology, Neo-Hinduism posits the modern, speculative academic notion of kathenotheism[21] in order to try to explain away the obviously discernable juxtaposition of a) the many lesser gods/goddesses of Sanatana Dharma contrasted against b) the clear concept of one ultimate and supreme God found in the Vedic scriptures.

Neo-Hindus repeatedly, and erroneously, claim that all of the gods and goddesses revealed in the Vedic scriptures are wholly and seamlessly interchangeable both with one another, as well as with Para-Brahman – the Supreme Absolute.[22]

---

[21] Sometimes also termed "henotheism".
[22] Indeed, contemporary New Age influenced Neo-Hindus will now go so far as to say that one can choose quite literally any being, person, object or thing (even a crystal, a rock or a

They claim that, despite the practically infinite degree of differences that are clearly observable between the various gods and goddesses in terms of their respective names, appearances, powers, stations, duties, lifespans, paraphernalia, clothes, personalities, back-stories, and the essential makeup of their very being, every one of these powerful beings are "ultimately" all one and the same, with no meaningful distinction between them. Very much akin to choosing one's favorite taste of ice cream, any single one of these various beings can be one's chosen flavor for worship and may be switched out at the slightest whim as the highest manifestation of the Absolute, in accordance with one's spiritual "taste".

Such kathenotheism, of course, is the very opposite of what traditional and authentic Sanatana Dharma

---

tree) as their personal object of worship or meditation, and that all such objects of veneration are equally valid expressions of the Supreme Absolute.

has always taught throughout its extremely long history. Again, Lord Krishna addresses the ideologically toxic pronouncements of Neo-Hindu kathenotheism in His *Bhagavad Gita.*

"Those who worship the demigods will take birth among the demigods; those who worship ghosts and spirits will take birth among such beings; those who worship ancestors go to the ancestors; and those who worship Me will live with Me." (*Bhagavad Gita*, 9.25)

Thus, God Himself makes it non-debatable and abundantly clear to us that, all objects of worship being radically distinct and different, we become like unto that which we meditate upon and worship. If we worship the *devas* and *devis*, we will be like unto them. If we worship ghosts, we will experience a tamasic outcome and have to live among the ghosts. If we worship the ancestors (*pitrs*), then we will be in their company. But if we worship God, then we will have the greatest of all spiritual attainments. We will enter Vaikuntha (the transcendental realm of God Himself) and be with Him forever. These diverse beings are not in any manner the same.

6) Rejection of "Idolatry" (*Murti* Worship)

Every single pre-Abrahamic religion in world history, bar none, engaged in the employment of sacred imagery as focal points of meditation and worship. This is especially the case with the most ancient, sophisticated and advanced of all ancient religions: Sanatana Dharma. Indeed, the very first religion to purposefully stray from this ancient and accepted norm of image worship was Judaism, then followed by the later Abrahamic religions of Christianity, Islam and Baha'ism.

While not all Neo-Hindus are united in the Abrahamically inspired error of straying away from *murti* worship, several historical Neo-Hindu movements did vigorously endeavor to introduce the Abrahamic dogma of anti-idolatry into the Vedic tradition. These were the Brahmo-samaj and the Arya-samaj, specifically. In doing so, these Abrahamic inspired movements separated themselves from the ancient norms of the Vedic tradition. They ceased to be Vedic.

7) Scientism: The Worship of Modern Science

Sanatana Dharma contains within it some of the most advanced scientific knowledge available to mankind, including in such fields as astronomy, biology, medicine, mathematics, physics, mechanics, engineering, genetics and epigenetics, etc. Vedic science, however, has next to nothing akin with the materialistic science of modernity.[23]

---

[23] The Natural Law based principles of Vedic science, for example, represent the very opposite principles of the modern empiricist school of Logical Positivism (founded in the late 1920s in Berlin and Vienna and led by such atheistic intellectuals as Moritz Schlick, Rudolf Carnap and Carl Hempel), which proposes that valid knowledge can only be

Modern scientific concerns, world-views or theoretical constructs did not exist in the Vedic scriptures; if only because modern science is too primitive in comparison to Vedic science.

Unlike the atheistically-inspired materialist sciences of modernity, the Vedic fields of science are dedicated to revealing science in a manner that is not at odds with or antithetical to nature, but that reflects nature perfectly. Vedic sciences work in harmony with natural cycles, forces, processes, axioms, ingredients and ethical principles in order to ensure that the resultant effects of all scientific endeavors are a boon to mankind rather than a curse. Scientism, on the other hand, views itself as being in a war to the death with the natural.[24]

---

derived from that which is empirically observable, and which forms one of the philosophical bases of Scientism.
[24] Intelligent people understand the efficacy of the scientific method. But no one of intelligence trusts the mainstream science anymore. Despite the wondrous "miracle of penicillin" and the fact that each proceeding generation of iPhones may (or may not) be a fraction better than the

Neo-Hinduism is a movement that has as its goal the taking of the very worst ideological blunders of modernity and attempting to graft them all unto the perfected frame of traditional Vedic culture. Early 19th century India witnessed both the importation of the zeitgeist of its historical time period, in which the insipid obviousness of the scientific method was still considered a revolutionary novelty throughout the British empire, coupled with the

---

> previous generation, mainstream science has caused at least as much harm, heartache, pain and nescience for humanity as it has good. From the mass death caused by the use of nuclear weaponry, to every single horrific development in the creation and improvement of armaments and weapons of war; from deadly chemical agents that have polluted every single aspect of our atmosphere, artificial agents that have poisoned our foods and rendered them free of all nutritional value, supposed pharmaceutical cures that contained wide arrays of side-affects that were worse than the original ailments, to deadly vaccinations forced upon the innocent public via mandates against their will and best interests, to fraudulent "research" that followed the money rather than the actual results of the scientific method; science was never the pristine and altruistic culture of knowledge that its fanatical devotees pretended that it was. Science has certainly contributed some good to the world as far as added conveniences. But it has, in actuality, added more suffering than good overall.

19th century Neo-Hindu enamoredness with all things that were non-Vedic. The result was that Neo-Hindus have incorporated into their psyches a ridiculously slavish adherence to Scientism – the vacuous worship of anything and everything that is termed "scientific". Neo-Hindus trust modern science; and nothing but the modern science.

Thus, in their puerile attempts at pleasing their Abrahamic/Modernist overlords and showing that "Hinduism" was on a par with the very latest progressive developments, Neo-Hindus began ransacking through the Vedic scriptures desperately seeking anything that might even remotely reflect the modern science of their day. In their lack of understanding of anything authentically Vedic, Neo-Hindus dream up apparitions of modern science behind every verse, concept and sacred story (*divya-katha*) to be found in the Vedic scriptures. Rather than relishing in the sweetness and wisdom of the overtly spiritual content of the

Vedic scriptures, all of which are overtly designed by God Himself to help us to know Him perfectly, Neo-Hindus see Darwinian evolution, ancient aliens and Einsteinian physics in our sacred scriptures instead.

8) Indologists and Atheist Academicians

It should not be surprising that the 19th century, the exact same era that spawned the new pseudo-religious concoction known as Neo-Hinduism, also gave birth to the grand era of "Indology". From that early era down to the present day, a stable of anti-Vedic and pro-Abrahamist/Globalist scholars, such as William Jones, Charles Wilkins, Max Muller, Romila Thapar, Michael Witzel, and Wendy Doniger, have been strategically placed as the academic gate-keepers on such fundamental questions as the actual origins, deepest meaning and social-political implications of Vedic civilization. Most significantly, these strategically placed gate-keepers are, to put it quite lightly, not in any manner friends of Sanatana Dharma, but rather very conscious, deliberative and zealous enemies.

It has been from the midst of such troublingly prejudiced and ideologically-driven salaried scholars that so many fabricated doctrinal hypotheses about Sanatana Dharma have arisen. Such dogmatic and absurdly unsupported theories include the now debunked "Aryan Invasion Theory" (AIT); the "Aryan Migration Theory"; the wholly arbitrary mis-dating of the dates of origination of each text of the Vedic scriptures and the dates of the lives of historically ancient *rishis* and personages in order to dishonestly make their dates of flourishing seem much more recent than they actually are;[25] the

---

[25] Only a few of the many examples of such purposeful mis-dating on the part of these anti-Vedic academicians include the unsubstantiated claims that the *Rig Veda* was first composed circa 1400 BC (the actual date is closer to 3800 BC); that the *Bhagavad Gita* can be dated no later than the 2nd century BC (the actual date is circa 3000 BC); that the twelve Vaishnava saints known as the Alvars flourished circa 5th -

relegating of all Vedic historical facts that contradict or imperil the supremacy of the Abrahamic/Modernist historical timeline as merely "mythology"; as well as the forced imposition of fraudulent Marxist, Feminist, Psychoanalytic, Deconstructionist and now LGBTQ "research methodologies" employed to caricature and grotesquely misrepresent the actual nature of the Vedic religion, rather than provide an honest and respectful assessment of the Vedic religion. In almost every field of academic concern, the dishonest and unprincipled "Indologists" and scholars of "South Asian Religion" have not hesitated to mischaracterize, denigrate and attack the foundations of the tradition of Sanatana Dharma at every turn.

Tragically, beginning from the very inception of the corrupt field of "Indology", Neo-Hindu thought

---

10th centuries AD (in actuality, they lived circa 4200 BC - 2700 BC).

leaders have enthusiastically embraced the anti-Vedic pronouncements of such disreputable "Indologists" as being the unassailable truth. No one adored the anti-Vedic "Indologists" with as much fervor as did the Neo-Hindus. Neo-Hindus have fully accepted the now discredited presumptions of the "Indologists" to heart even at a time when the rest of the Western world no longer takes their ideas all that seriously anymore! Indeed, Neo-Hindus embrace such anti-Vedic professors as Max Muller as being historically among the greatest friends of Sanatana Dharma, rather than acknowledging that such "Indologists" as Max Muller and his ilk were never benefactors of Sanatana Dharma, but were, in fact, anti-Vedic fiends.

9) Acceptance of the Qualitative Evolutionary Hypothesis

One of the utmost domineering dogmatic edifices

of Scientism that has been especially latched onto with the greatest tenacity since the 19th century has been the Darwinian theory of evolution. Since the first publication of Charles Darwin's seminal work *On the Origin of Species* in 1859, the theory of qualitative evolution has become one of the theoretical bedrocks of modern atheism and Scientism.[26] Qualitative evolutionism is seen in such concepts as: the actual biological evolutionary theories that Darwin primarily espoused, but then leading historically to eventual Social Darwinism, as well as the Marxist inspired political ideology of Progressivism.

---

[26] Arguably, the notion of qualitative evolution can first be traced to the German philosopher Georg William Friedrich Hegel's (1770-1831) notion that history represents a progressive and ever upwardly mobile evolution of the consciousness of freedom. Such progression is purportedly fueled by the engine of Hegel's dialectical method of Thesis/Antithesis/Synthesis. Thus, history, for Hegel progresses from the stages of the primitive, to the qualitative heights of civilization (which was, of course, Germanic Lutheran civilization in Hegel's mind).

In broad-spectrum terms, qualitative evolutionism postulates the notion that human societies throughout history have evolved both biologically, as well as (and most importantly) in all the finer aspects of internal human culture. Qualitative evolutionism hypothesizes the idea that humans have become progressively better (i.e., increasingly superior) in their inherent qualities than was the case with previous generations in such internal facets as aesthetic refinement, ethics and virtue, intelligence and logic, compassion and empathy, etiquette and propriety, as well as personal tastes, "social awareness", and even hygiene.

To state the case for qualitative evolutionism in brevis: the idea of qualitative evolutionists is that, the further back one goes in time, necessarily and correspondingly, the stupider, more primitive, more violent and more unrefined human beings were in every important psychological, behavioral and cultural aspect of their lives. We denizens of the current era presently represent the very apex of all human 'spiritual' and cultural achievements! Additionally, as time progresses forward from our present era, humans, and consequently human society, will of necessity continue to evolve qualitatively to higher and higher states of superiority. The cataclysmically destructive social, theological, political, psychological and cultural impact of the ideology of qualitative evolutionism, from its 19th century inception up to the very present moment, cannot be overstated.

Disastrously, almost every major figure in the history of the formation of Neo-Hinduism, and up to this very day, enthusiastically supported the devastating dogma of qualitative evolution.[27]

---

[27] One of the most influential of these Neo-Hindu doyens, as only one example, was the pseudo-*guru* Aurobindo (1872-1950), who fully embraced the theories of Darwinian evolution as a result of the influence of his father, who was himself a member of the Brahmo Samaj. The Brahmo Samaj being, in turn, one of the very earliest of Neo-Hindu movements in India.

Leaders of Neo-Hinduism speak frantically and repeatedly of the inevitable and involuntary "evolution" of global society into an eventual "oneness" (as do their New Age descendants today). They have all thoroughly accepted with zealous, semi-religious adherence all of the divisions of geologic time and historical periods[28] invented by atheistic evolutionists.

Indeed, many Neo-Hindu leaders have been so tragically indoctrinated by the theories of qualitative evolutionism to the point of postulating the drastically anti-Vedic and adharmic (anti-Dharmic) heresy that the *avataras* (incarnations) of Sriman Narayana represent nothing more significant than biological evolutionism in a mythologically prescient symbolic form! Keshub Chandra Sen, one of Neo-Hinduism's most important developers and leaders, stated the following in this regard in a

---

[28] Such as the Hadean, Archean, Proterozoic, Phanerozoic, Palaeozoic, Mesozoic, Cenozoic, etc., etc., eras.

public lecture:

> "Lo! the Hindu Avatar rises from the lowest scale of life through the fish, the tortoise, and the hog up to the perfection of humanity. Indian Avatarism is, indeed, a **crude representation**[29] of the ascending scale of Divine creation. Such precisely is the modern theory of evolution. How from the lowest forms of gross matter is evolved the vitality of the vegetable world in all its fulness and luxuriance! And then from the most perfect and vital types of vegetable life springs the least in the animal kingdom, which again rises through endless and growing varieties, to the very highest in intelligence and sagacity. But creation stops not here. From animal life it ascends to humanity, and finds its full development in man. In the evolution of man, however, creation is not exhausted. It goes farther and farther still, along the course of progressive humanity." (*Keshub Chunder Sen's Lectures in India*, pg. 13)

In their unwittingly oblivious stampede to wholly embrace Scientism, evolutionism and Modernity,

---

[29] My emphasis.

Neo-Hindu leaders have even thrown God Himself into their dumpster of "archaic Hindu savagery" in their eager desire to exorcise Sanatana Dharma of any authentic spiritual content or connection to its actual roots in the Vedic scriptures and tradition. The early Neo-Hindus, especially, thought that they were being sophisticated and urbane in slavishly copying their Christian and modern scientist masters' ridicule of Sanatana Dharma; instead, they were just being nothing more than cowardly anti-Vedic quislings.

Qualitative evolutionism is, of course, one of the easiest of claims to defeat since it can be cursorily disproven via an objective and empirical observation of modifications within the essential qualities of both individual human beings, as well as the resulted cultures and societies of such human beings, over the span of known time. Not only do we witness, for example, many hundreds of civilizations throughout ancient history that were in every manner qualitatively superior to anything ever produced by modernity, but we can even witness the qualitative devolution of man (behaviorally, culturally, spiritually, intellectually, sapiently, morally, etc.) even in just the last few decades of the current era (i.e., the 20th and 21st centuries). Rap entertainers are infinitely substandard in their "poetic" compositional output in comparison to a Shakespeare or a Kali Dasa. "Cardi B" is no Bach. And are we going to argue with a straight face that public etiquette, politeness, civic responsibility and compassion are more evolved in the 21st century than they were even just a few generations ago?

The Vedic critique of qualitative evolutionism having now been understood, it is important to also understand that there is a marked difference between the dogma of qualitative evolution versus the principle of natural selection. Qualitative evolution and natural selection are not the same. While the authentic and *Veda*-based tradition of

Sanatana Dharma thoroughly rejects the specious theory of qualitative evolution, the principle of natural selection is, on the other hand, both accepted and annunciated in the Vedic tradition.

The principle of natural selection, concisely stated, is the empirically observable fact that, within any specific species or grouping of living entities, those individuals of the specific like-grouping who are in possession of those skills and attributes necessary to survive will have a statistically higher probability of passing on their genetic makeup to the next generation. The passing on of these specific, successful genes will then lead to the increased prominence of those genes in future generations. This general concept of natural selection, i.e., that genetic alterations take place in a given species from one generation to another, is upheld in Sanatana Dharma as a biological manifestation of natural law (Dharma).

Where Sanatana Dharma differs with the Darwinian theory of evolution is that, while Vedic scholars understand that natural selection leads to an alteration in proceeding generations of any given species, qualitative evolutionism takes an empirically unsupported leap outside the bounds of actual science by claiming that such natural selection leads to not merely *alteration*, but to necessarily *qualitative evolutionary* (i.e., superior) changes. According to qualitative evolutionism, every genetic alteration is necessarily a qualitatively ***superior*** alteration. Sanatana Dharma readily acknowledges intergenerational genetic alterations; but qualitative evolutionism additionally states – and on no other "evidence" than politically-fueled blind faith – that such genetic alterations are necessarily better and more superior with every proceeding generation. Of this belief on the part of the qualitative evolutionist, there is zero proof or evidence.

Indeed, the vastly deeper Vedic understanding of the process of natural selection is that those behavioral attributes that lead to biological dominance are, in actuality, often antithetical to qualitatively desirable attributes. Those beings who are more likely to thrive in a viciously competitive natural environment, and who are thus more likely to pass on their genetic inheritance to future generations, are those beings who themselves tend to be more vicious, more violent, more unforgiving, more forceful, more irrational, more selfish, more cunning and conniving (as opposed to wise), and more aggressive in general. Those beings who, on the other hand, possess qualitatively superior attributes such as compassion, empathy, patience, reason, inner calm, wisdom, the impetus to help others, etc., are often those beings who, more likely than not, do not necessarily survive to pass on their genetic makeup to future generations.

As a personal recollection to better illustrate the above principle, I recall being in an excellently taught history course when I was an undergraduate student. The professor had just explained to us how in Medieval Europe during the Black Plague, many of the very qualitatively finest people in society – nuns, priests, monks, students, religious laypeople and healers – all selflessly rushed into the very centers of the plague zones to try to help the sick and dying, while the rest of the locals were simultaneously rushing out of these same areas as quickly as their feet or mules could transport them.

Sadly, the majority of these spiritual/intellectual elites of society perished in their attempts to do good, while the cowardly and self-centered tended to survive. The qualitatively best of society who perished would not live to pass on their qualitatively superior genes to future generations, while the qualitatively inferior genes were guaranteed to remain with society. When the professor paused in her lesson in melancholy reflection of the story she had just told, I raised my hand and commented. "So what we witness in such situations is a type of survival of the **un**fit." The professor nodded in agreement. In many cases of altruism, the resultant effect from a natural selection perspective is not only that the qualitative evolution of the species is not the end result, but the qualitative devolution of the species is what we empirically witness.

The fact of such historical devolution in the quality of human beings is (not surprising to anyone but Neo-Hindus) perfectly in keeping with the Vedic principle of *yugas* (ages), in which it is understood that humanity has been continuously devolving over the course of a repeated cycle of ages. We are currently in the most devolved of ages, the Kali Yuga. The Dharmic principle of natural selection is one of the array of engines that brings about the continued devolution of humanity that in turn leads to the continued devolution of each *yuga*. Given that the Vedic understanding of natural selection is predicated upon actual empirical evidence, and not merely blind faith, and that such empirical evidence supports the teachings of Sanatana Dharma, the Vedic scientific method is superior in its explicative processes to that of both qualitative evolution and of the scientific methodological models that are found within the context of Modernity.

10) Neo-Hinduism is Aligned with Western Liberalism and Globalism

From the time of its coming into being, up to the very present hour, Neo-Hinduism has always consciously and deliberately aligned itself with the ideological forces and tendencies of Western liberalism, progressivism, leftism, socialism and globalism. As will be detailed especially in the next chapter, the early founders of Neo-Hinduism derived almost all of their foundational ideas from the dismal legacy of the European Enlightenment era (1685-1815), and from the most liberal ideological crazes of the early 19th century. The *"gurus"* of the earliest Neo-Hindus were not Vyasa, Narada, Patanjali or Ramanuja. Rather, the direct mentors and advisors of these early apostate "reformers" of the traditional religion of India were imported representatives of the most extreme liberal sociopolitical movements of their era. The Western advisors of the nascent Neo-Hindu movement were all either Unitarians, Universalists, liberal Christian pastors, Freemasons, Globalists, atheists, or in several cases a dizzying combination thereof.

The unnatural alignment of Neo-Hinduism with Western liberal ideologies continued into the late 19th and early 20th century with the forced merger of socialism and sundry crypto-Marxist elements into many aspects of Neo-Hinduism, coupled with the nascent New Age influence of the Theosophical movement.[30] The formal marriage of Neo-Hinduism and liberalism came about, however, in the late 1960s in America and Europe, with the morally debauched and leftwing hippie movement misappropriating many elements of Vedic spirituality, sometimes with, but more often without, attribution.

Hippies began gleefully adopting many of, what they perceived to be, the more exotic elements of the Vedic tradition with neither a deep knowledge of, nor respect for the many sacred teachings and practices that they were now thoughtlessly toying with. As a causal result of this incongruous jumble of "Hindu" spirituality, coupled with the free sex, drugs, celebration of irrationality, relativism, New Age magic(k)al thinking, and disastrous leftist political movements of the 1960s, today Sanatana

---

[30] One of the prime examples being Annie Besant (1847-1933), the radical leftist, socialist, feminist and irredeemable globalist who became the leader of the Theosophical Society from 1907-1933.

Dharma has the distasteful and exceedingly inaccurate reputation of being itself a liberal and hippie culture. It is not.

There is absolutely nothing even remotely leftwing or hippyish about Sanatana Dharma. Such concepts and practices as *karma*, Yoga, *chakras*, *kundalini*, vegetarianism, Ayurveda (the natural medicinal system of Sanatana Dharma) and sitars have exactly zero to do with hippies, the New Age phenomenon, leftwing movements or liberalism. These concepts and practices are exclusively Vedic. Sociopolitical liberalism is the very antithesis of everything that Sanatana Dharma stands for and teaches.

Actual Sanatana Dharma is exceedingly and unapologetically pro-family, pro-morality, pro-freedom, pro-life, as well as completely anti-degeneracy, anti-socialist, anti-abortion, and in every other manner radically traditional. The enormous disservice that fraudulent Neo-Hindu leaders and their Western liberal puppet-masters have forced upon Sanatana Dharma has only served to ruin the reputation of the Vedic tradition in the minds of untold generations of people, both in the Western world and in India. It is my hope that this present book, as well as all of my other works, will serve to bring about the restoration of Sanatana Dharma's unassailable reputation.

11) Neo-Hinduism, Symbolism and Mythology

Yet another common element of Neo-Hinduism is the overly employed tendency of Neo-Hindu supremos to reduce traditional elements from the Vedic scriptures, sacred stories (*divya-katha*) and Vedic history to the academic and pseudo-psychological realm of myth and symbolism.

The related terms "myth", "mythology", "mythological", etc., have had an interesting history and a very pointed polemic use in academic discourse on Sanatana Dharma. That the terms are rife with very negative connotations is doubted by very few. The way the terms are used today both within academia, as well as by the general public, is to denote something that is untrue, false, a lie, "primitive" (i.e., not of Modernity). The ultimate question that all followers of Sanatana Dharma need to ask is: is it really of any intellectual necessity that such a powerfully negative term as "myth" also be associated with the sacred stories, teachings, scriptures and history of Sanatana Dharma?

Polemically speaking, one culture's "myth" is another culture's sacred history...and vice versa. The academic field of the study of "mythological" literature was founded by 18th century European Classicists who took their simplistic misconceptions about their own Greco-Roman, pre-Christian religious and cultural heritage, and attempted to then graft these misconceptions onto all contemporary non-Christian cultures - including that of Sanatana Dharma. These founders of "mythology" studies - including such individuals as Sir George Grey, Rudolph Otto and Karl Kerenyi - were convinced, as is unarguably evident in their writings, that the entire realm of religious story could be clearly demarcated into two radically distinct camps: Myth and History.

A) The first category is "Myth" proper, that is: the "primitive" stories about gods, goddesses, spirits, demons, magic and mysticism, etc. found throughout all of the "Pagan"[31] pre-Christian and non-Biblical cultures of the world. Such stories are all considered to be certainly no more than the ignorant "pre-scientific" attempts of "primitive" peoples (*their* precise wording) to come to terms

---

[31] Which demonstrably includes the Vedic civilization and all the elements thereof.

with and explain such frightening mysteries as natural weather phenomena.[32] The study of such woefully mythologically ridden cultures was then relegated by these supposed mythology authorities to the nascent fields of anthropology, folk-lore studies, ethnic studies, religious studies, and art history studies. The "myths" of all non-Abrahamic cultures were thus falsely portrayed as being archaic, primitive, and not worthy of serious scholarly study.

B) The second category that religious stories were placed in was termed "History", that is: Biblical literature and all supposedly factual accounts of events proceeding such literature to be found throughout the history of the modern West.[33] Whereas, for example, stories about Rama as the

---

[32] The stereotypical scenario offered by these atheistic scholars is that the inexplicable spectacle of lightning and thunder left our ancestors trembling in worshipful fear!
[33] The histories of non-Western peoples and nations, too, were only allowed to be viewed through the ideologically myopic lens of post-Enlightenment era Modernity.

Dharma-raja (Dharmic King) of Ayodhya were considered to be no more than quaint heroic myths, for example, stories of Moses parting the Red Sea were accepted as being thoroughly and concretely historical. This was the case even though there is more archeological and textual evidence for the former than for the latter being actual historical facts.

In order to study these supposed historical facts about Abrahamic culture, modern atheist scholars employed a very different battery of academic disciplines entirely, including philosophical, ethical, literary, psychological, etc. The only overlapping exception to this biased division of study into "myth" versus "history" being the field of philology, which was employed to research both the "glorious history" of the Abrahamic world, as well as the "primitive utterings" of the *Ṛg Veda*. Apparently, according to the academia of Modernity, only the "history" of Abrahamic Man is a worthy enough subject for liberal arts study, philosophical consideration, and serious intellectual analysis.

There is the wonderful saying that we have all encountered that assures us that "history" is written by the victors of inter-cultural conflict, by the conquerors. Since the very inception of the Abrahamist/Modernist/Globalist Neo-Hindu movement, Neo-Hindu leaders have acquiesced the mythological studies approach of their anti-Vedic puppet masters completely and without question. Neo-Hinduism thus represents nothing more than the conquering and colonization of the Vedic mind by an alien world-view that seeks its slow, yet complete, eventual destruction.

In the mind of the typical Neo-Hindu, all of the sacred stories of the Vedic scriptures, including the histories of Lord Sri Rama, Lord Sri Krishna, the sacred *rishis*, Chakravartins, Dharma-rajas, etc. are to be relegated to mere mythology. On the other hand, even the mostly improvable stories of the Garden of Eden, Noah's Ark, Abraham, Moses, the Judges, King David, etc. are unquestioningly accepted by most Neo-Hindu leaders, *"gurus"* and historians as being incontrovertible and established fact. This is the case even though the evidence for these Biblical, supposed historical facts are in many cases infinitely less strong than the evidence supporting the historicity of the ancient stories of Sanatana Dharma.

What many Neo-Hindu leaders called the "mythical" Sarasvati River, for example, was later discovered to be a tangible geological fact in the 20th century by no less empirical evidence than satellite photography. Krishna's "mythological" city of Dvaraka was, likewise, impertinently discovered off the coast of Gujarat in 1963 (anyone out there have a crane?). The supposed "myths" of the

Shastras seem to have the incorrigible and repeated habit of consistently allowing themselves to be proven factual by physical empirical evidence.

Neo-Hindu leaders have committed an enormous disservice to the Vedic tradition in their eagerness to feign sophistication before the eyes of their Abrahamic masters by relegating all of the most important historical figures and occurrences recorded throughout the Vedic scriptures to the bin of "mythology". Such terms as "myth" should be absolutely anathema to every sincere and self-respecting follower of Sanatana Dharma when speaking about our sacred stories. Let us all be in agreement that these sacred stories of Sanatana Dharma must never again be degraded by terming them "myth".

The inherent dignity, strength, nobility, and beauty of traditional Sanatana Dharma was recognized as the foremost threat to Christian European rule in South Asia. The mendaciously strategic invention of Neo-Hinduism by the enemies of Sanatana Dharma was the response. Had the colonialist/globalist program to eradicate authentic, traditional Sanatana Dharma been carried out with a British face, it would not have been met with as much success as it did. Therefore, an Indian face was used to impose Neo-Hinduism upon the Vedic people. The resultant effects of the activities of Indian Neo-Hindus were ruinous for traditional and authentic Sanatana Dharma, and the painful repercussions of this subversion are being felt to this very day. The primary dilemma within the Vedic community as we find it today is, in a nutshell, the following two problems:

1) Not recognizing that there are really two distinct and conflicting Vedic communities today: a) Traditionalist Sanatana Dharma and b) Neo-Hinduism.

2) While leaders of traditionalist Sanatana Dharma are the guardians of authentic Vedic religion, both philosophically, in practice, and attitudinally, they have only very recently[34] come fully to grips with the many challenges (as much covert as overt challenges) to traditional Sanatana Dharma that the modern world has presented. Traditionalists have only recently been successful in negotiating authentic Vedic Dharma with an ability to interface with modernity and communicate this unadulterated Vedic Dharma in a way that the modern mind can most appreciate it.

---

[34] Specifically with the birth of the International Sanatana Dharma Society, a movement introduced to the world in 1998, the goal of which is the full restoration of traditional and authentic Vedic religion, culture and civilization in every sphere of human concern.

The contemporary Vedic community will continue to be mired in confusion about its own true meaning and value until all the many poisons of Neo-Hinduism can be finally eradicated from its midst. In order to accomplish this restoration of authentic Sanatana Dharma, Vedic traditionalists must assertively, professionally and intelligently communicate the reality of genuine Sanatana Dharma to the world. We thus call upon all sincere followers of authentic and orthodox Sanatana Dharma to fully support the efforts of the International Sanatana Dharma Society in its mission to restore the authentic Vedic tradition throughout every corner of the world. Until this is accomplished, Neo-Hinduism will continue its destructive campaign of presenting itself as an actual representative of the Vedic religion, while simultaneously subverting the very Vedic religion it falsely claims to represent.

Chapter Nine: The Non-Vedic Origins of Radical Universalism

Radical Universalism is neither traditionally Vedic, nor classically Vedic in its origins. The origins of the distinctly non-Vedic idea of Radical Universalism, and the direct paralyzing impact it has had on modern Vedic (i.e., "Hindu") philosophy, can only be traced back to the early 19th century. Radical Universalism is a fallacious theory that is only slightly older than two centuries, yet the results of which have been devastating for both the progress of serious Vedic philosophical expression since the 19th century, as well as in its practical effect of severely undermining the self-esteem of many modern Indian Hindus. Its intellectual roots are not to be found in Sanatana Dharma itself, but rather are clearly traced back to the attempts of both highly liberal Christian missionaries, as well as Freemason-inspired enthusiasts of the burgeoning globalism of the British empire to alter the genuine teachings of authentic Sanatana Dharma.

Radical Universalism was the vogue among 19th century, British educated Indians, most of who had very little reliably authentic information about their own Vedic intellectual and spiritual heritage. These westernized and highly cosmopolitan Indians were often overly eager to gain acceptance and respectability for themselves and for their "reformed" version of Indian culture from a Christian globalist European audience who perceived in Sanatana Dharma nothing more than the childish prattle of a brutish and subjugated, colonized people.

Many exaggerated and concocted stereotypes about Vedic civilization had been unsettling impressionable European minds for a century previous to their era. Rather than attempting to assertively refute these many stereotypes about

Vedic culture by presenting Sanatana Dharma in its authentic and pristine form, however, many of these 19th century Christianized and globalized Indians felt it was necessary to, instead, gut Sanatana Dharma of anything that might seem offensively exotic to the European mind. Radical Universalism seemed to be the perfect base-notion upon which to artificially construct a "new" "Hinduism" that would give the Anglicized 19th century Indian intelligentsia the acceptability they so yearned to be granted by their British masters.

We encounter one of the first instances of the Radical Universalist infiltration into Sanatana Dharma in the syncretistic teachings of Ram Mohan Roy (1772-1833), the founder of the infamous Brahmo Samaj. A highly controversial figure during his life, Roy was a Bengali pseudo-intellectual who was heavily influenced by the teachings of the Unitarian Church, a heterodox and liberal extremist denomination of Christianity.[35] In addition to studying Christianity, Islam and some Sanskrit, he studied Hebrew and Greek with the dream of translating the Bible into Bengali.

A self-described Vedic "reformer", he viewed Sanatana Dharma through a warped colonial Christian lens. The Christian missionaries had told Roy that traditional Sanatana Dharma was a barbaric and archaic religion that had led to the mass oppression, superstition and ignorance of the Indian people. He believed them. More, Roy saw Biblical teachings, specifically, as holding the cherished key to altering traditional Vedic teachings to make it more palatable to India's colonial masters.

---

[35] Indeed, in 1961 the Unitarian Church (the history of which stretches back to 16th century Europe) was to officially merge with another denomination quite literally named the Universalist Church (originally formed in 1793). The resulting denomination is now known as the Unitarian Universalist Association (UUA).

In his missionary zeal to Christianize the Vedic religion, this passionate "reformer" even wrote an anti-Vedic, radically pro-Christian tract, aimed at converting followers of Sanatana Dharma to Christianity, known as *The Precepts of Jesus: The Guide to Peace and Happiness*.[36] In it, he makes many impassioned appeals to his "fellow Hindus" to open their hearts to the message of Christianity.

> "In my present vindication of the unity of the Deity, as revealed through the writings of the Old and New Testaments, I appeal not only to those who sincerely believe in the books of revelation, and make them the standard of their faith and practice, and who must, therefore, deeply feel the great importance of the divine oracles being truly interpreted; but I also appeal to those who, although indifferent about religion, yet devote their minds to the investigation and discovery of truth, and who will, therefore, not think it unworthy of their attention to

---

[36] The most recent edition of this silly screed is now available in a 2018 edition of 352 pages, ISBN number: 0266722946.

> ascertain what are the genuine doctrines of Christianity…" (*The Precepts of Jesus: The Guide to Peace and Happiness*, pg. 328)

It was directly from these Christian missionaries that Roy derived the bulk of his ideas, including the anti-Vedic idea of the radical equality of all religions. Ram Mohan Roy's faith and devotion to Christianity was so personal that he wrote enthusiastically about his plans to devote himself to publishing a periodical dedicated to Biblical studies.

> "As Christianity is happily not a subject resting on vague metaphysical speculations, but is founded upon the authority of books written in languages which are understood and explained according to known and standing rules, I therefore propose, with a view to the more speedy and certain attainment of religious truth, to establish a monthly periodical publication, commencing from the month of April next, to be devoted to Biblical Criticism, and to subject Unitarian as well as Trinitarian doctrines to the test of fair argument, if those of the latter persuasion will consent

> thus to submit the scriptural grounds on which their tenets concerning the Trinity are built." (*The Precepts of Jesus: The Guide to Peace and Happiness*, pg. 330)

In addition to acquiring Radical Universalism from the Christian missionaries, Roy also felt it necessary to Christianize Sanatana Dharma by adopting many fundamentalist Biblical theological beliefs into his new Neo-Hindu "reform" movement. Some of these other non-intrinsic adaptations included a rejection of Vedic panentheistic monotheism, to be substituted with a more Biblical notion of anthropomorphic monotheism; a rejection of all iconic *murti* worship ("graven images" as the crypto-Christian supporters of the Brahmo Samaj phrased it); and a repudiation of the doctrine of *avataras*, or the divine descent of God.

Roy's immediate successors, Debendranath Tagore (1817-1905) and Keshub Chandra Sen (1838-1884), attempted to incorporate even more Christian ideals into this new invention of "Neo-Hinduism".[37] Sen even went so far as concocting a Brahmo Samaj text that contained passages from a variety of differing religious traditions, including Jewish, Christian, Muslim, Hindu, and Buddhist in his attempt to bolster the newly concocted theory that all religions were the same. Continuing Ram Mohan Roy's Christian-inspired tirade against Vedic "idolatry", Sen railed against *murti* worship with the zeal of an Evangelical Christian preacher! In one of his preserved lectures, he treacherously advises Christian missionaries on the very best tactics to convert followers of Sanatana Dharma to Christianity!

> "Believe this, ye who wish to be true and loyal to Jesus Christ. And to you, ambassadors of Christ in India, let me say a word of warning. India is sick of idolatry.

---

[37] Sen, specifically, became a member of Freemasonry in 1855 under the auspices of the Goodwill Fraternity lodge, which was founded by the Unitarian Reverend Charles Dall. He also studied Christianity with the Reverend James Long, among other anti-Vedic Christian missionaries.

Add not to the already overcrowded pantheon of Hindu gods and goddesses a fresh divinity in the name of Jesus. Never say Christ is the very God of the universe, the Father of all mankind. If you preach 'him crucified' as your very Father, you preach idolatry and heresy. The early Fathers are against you. Holy Writ is against you. Christ too is against you. Therefore, shun this hideous lie of Christ the Father, and preach Christ the Son. Tell our people distinctly that Christ is not an incarnation like the myriad deities worshipped in this land. If you do not, you incur the tremendous risk of poisoning a whole nation with new forms of idolatry. Beware. Remember you accept a terrible responsibility in preaching to the Hindu people." (*Keshub Chunder Sen's Lectures in India*, pg. 37)

Keshub Chandra Sen, one of the most important developers of the entire movement of Neo-Hinduism was nothing less (and nothing more) than an enabler of Christian missionary activity aimed as converting the "idol worshipping Hindus" to his newly adopted faith of Christianity. Thus, he was a conscious and deliberate enemy of Sanatana

Dharma, not a "reformer".

In his later years, Sen portrayed himself as a divinized Old Testament style prophet of the "New Dispensation", which he felt replaced the Old and New Testaments, in addition to supplanting traditional Sanatana Dharma. In a speech Sen delivered in 1866, he publicly proclaimed that "India would be for Christ alone who already stalks the land."[38] In other words, Keshub Chandra Sen initiated a project to create a new religion that would replace traditional Sanatana Dharma with a Christian-inspired, globalist and Radical Universalist religious fabrication.

With Sen's continued descent into anti-Vedic apostasy and megalomania, the movement rapidly declined in importance and influence. The Brahmo

---

[38] Chisholm, Hugh, ed. (1911). "Keshub Chunder Sen". *Encyclopædia Britannica*. Vol. 15 (11th ed.). Cambridge University Press. p. 760.

Samaj is today extinct as an organization, but the global Vedic community is still feeling the damaging effects of its pernicious influence even at present.

The next two Neo-Hindu Radical Universalists that we witness in the history of 19th century Sanatana Dharma are Ramakrishna (1836-1886) and Vivekananda (1863-1902). Though Vivekananda was a disciple (*shishya*) of Ramakrishna, the two led very different lives. Ramakrishna was born into a family within the tradition of Sanatana Dharma in Dakshineshwar. In his adult life, he was a Vedic temple priest and a fervently demonstrative devotee of the Divine Mother. His primary object of worship was the goddess Kali, whom he worshipped with intense devotion all of his life.

Despite his initial Vedic roots, however, many of Ramakrishna's foundational ideas and practices were derived, not from the ancient wisdom of classical Sanatana Dharma, but from the non-Vedic religious outlooks of Islam, liberal Christianity and 19th century globalism. Though he saw himself as being primarily Dharmi, Ramakrishna also resorted to worshipping in mosques and churches, and believed that all religions aimed at the same supreme destination. He experimented with Muslim, Christian, and a wide variety of Vedic practices, blending, mixing and matching practices and beliefs as they appealed to him at any given moment.

As he himself recounts his first experiments with Radical Universalism, Ramakrishna states:

> "I have practised all religions—Hinduism, Islam, Christianity—and I have also followed the paths of the different Hindu sects. I have found that it is the same God toward whom all are directing their steps, though along different paths. You must try all beliefs and traverse all the different ways

once. Wherever I look, I see men quarrelling in the name of religion—Hindus, Mohammedans, Brahmos, Vaishnavas, and the rest. But they never reflect that He who is called Krishna is also called Siva, and bears the name of the Primal Energy, Jesus, and Allah as well—the same Rama with a thousand names..."[39]

In 1875, Ramakrishna met the crypto-Christian Keshub Chandra Sen, who was the then leader of the Neo-Hindu Brahmo Samaj, and formed a very close working relationship with the self-proclaimed prophet of the "New Dispensation". Sen introduced Ramakrishna to the close-knit community of Neo-Hindu activists who lived in Calcutta, and would in turn often bring these crypto-Christian Neo-Hindu activists to Ramakrishna's *satsanghas*.

---

[39] Rolland, Romain (1929). "The Return to Man". *The Life of Ramakrishna*. pp. 49-62.

Throughout his colorful and short life, Ramakrishna remained a functional near-illiterate. He never studied, nor was capable of even reading, any of the Vedic literature, the epistemological foundation of all spiritual knowledge in the tradition of Sanatana Dharma. He was wholly unfamiliar with both classical Vedic literature and philosophy, as well as the authentic philosophical teachings of the great *Acharyas* who served as the preceptor-guardians of those sacred teachings.

Despite the severely obvious challenges that he experienced in understanding even the very basics of Vedic theology, playing upon the en vogue sentiment of religious universalism of his day, Ramakrishna ended up being one of the most widely popular of Neo-Hindu Radical Universalists. The fame of Ramakrishna was to be soon eclipsed, however, by that of his most famous disciple.

Swami Vivekananda was arguably by far Ramakrishna's most capable disciple. An eloquent and charismatic speaker, Vivekananda will be forever honored by the Vedic community for his brilliant defense of Sanatana Dharma at the Parliament of World Religions gathering of liberal religious leaders that occurred in Chicago in 1893. Likewise, Vivekananda contributed greatly to the revival of interest in the study of Vedic scriptures and philosophy in turn-of-the-century India. The positive contributions of Vivekananda toward spreading at least a basic knowledge of Sanatana Dharma throughout the world are numerous and great indeed.

Notwithstanding his remarkable preaching undertakings, however, Vivekananda found himself in a similarly difficult position as other Neo-Hindu leaders of his day were in; how to make sense of the ancient ways of Sanatana Dharma, and hopefully preserve at least some semblance of

Sanatana Dharma, in the face of the overwhelming onslaught of secular modernity? Like other Neo-Hindu leaders before him, Vivekananda found himself at a complete loss in creating a successful interface of Sanatana Dharma and modernity.

Despite some positive contributions by Vivekananda and other Neo-Hindus in attempting to formulate a Vedic response to the many challenges of modernity, that response was often made at the direct expense of authentic Vedic teachings. All such attempts at a fruitful interface only led to calamitous compromises of the purity of Sanatana Dharma at the sacrificial altar of modern materialism. Vivekananda, along with the other leaders of the Neo-Hindu movement, felt it was necessary to both water down the authentic Sanatana Dharma of their ancestors, and to adopt such anti-Vedic impulses as Radical Universalism, with the hope of gaining the approval of the European masters they found ruling over them.

Vivekananda differed quite significantly from his famous *guru* in many ways, including in his educational background, philosophical outlook, personal style, and organizational ambitions. While Ramakrishna led a contemplative life of relative isolation from the larger world, Vivekananda was to become a celebrated figure on the world religion stage. Vivekananda frequently took a somewhat dismissive attitude toward traditional Vedic culture as it was practiced in his day, arguing (quite incorrectly) that Sanatana Dharma was too often irrational, overly mythologically oriented, and too divorced from the more practical need for social welfare work.[40]

---

[40] The religion and culture of Sanatana Dharma has always encouraged its followers to offer charity, compassion and assistance to the poor and needy in society. Indeed, Christianity and the Abrahamic religions have no precedent claim to fame in their charitable work in comparison to the charity traditionally dispensed by Vedic institutions and persons. However, the 19th century saw the birth of a Marxist, Socialist and radically egalitarian inspired form of social welfare work that was specifically based upon secular-materialist politics and which was inherently foreign to traditional Sanatana Dharma. Sadly, one of the additional

He was not very interested in Ramakrishna's earlier emphasis on mystical devotion and ecstatic worship. Rather, Vivekananda laid stress on the centrality of his own idiosyncratic and universalistic approach to Vedanta, what later came to be known as "Neo-Vedanta".[41] Vivekananda's take on Radical Universalism differed slightly with Ramakrishna's version of Radical Universalism by attempting to superimpose a distinctly neo-Vedantic outlook to the idea of the unity of all religions. Vivekananda advocated a sort of hierarchical Radical Universalism that espoused the equality of all religions, while simultaneously claiming that all

---

foundational dogmas of the Neo-Hindu movement was to offer knee-jerk support to such Marxist oriented "social justice" projects. Vivekananda was among such misled Neo-Hindus.

[41] Neo-Vedanta later went on to be one of the foundational pillars of the modern New Age movement. Neo-Vedanta has come to be known as the spiritually vapid "non-dualism" phenomenon in very recent decades throughout North America and Europe, which consists of multiple hundreds of exceedingly unknowledgeable and entrepreneurial "satsang" leaders who charge their audiences fees for talks consisting of pithy New Age adages mixed with a small degree of neo-Vedantic insipidity.

religions are really evolving from inferior notions of religiosity to a pinnacle mode.[42] That pinnacle of all religious thought and practice was, for Vivekananda, of course Neo-Hinduism. Though Vivekananda contributed a great deal toward helping European and American non-Dharmis to understand the greatness of some aspects of Sanatana Dharma, the Radical Universalist and Neo-Hindu inaccuracies that he fostered have also done a great deal of harm as well.

---

[42] Yet another ideological offspring of secular-materialist modernity that has been eagerly and enthusiastically adopted by the Neo-Hindu movement is Darwinian evolution. Many Neo-Hindus have thoroughly fallen for the anti-Vedic and erroneous premise that humanity has, since its very inception and throughout the entirety of its history, been undergoing a mostly straightforward, linear progression of qualitative evolution. This, despite all empirical and historical evidence pointing toward the very opposite conclusion, and (more importantly) despite the fact that the Vedic scriptures teach the very opposite of qualitative evolution. Sanatana Dharma actually teaches the reality of qualitative devolution.

In order to fully experience the multitude of gifts that Sanatana Dharma offers us in its most spiritually evocative and philosophically compelling form, we must learn to recognize, and reject, the concocted influences of Neo-Hinduism that have permeated the whole of Vedic thought today. It is now time to rid ourselves of the liberal Christian and secular globalist inspired "reformism" that so deeply prejudiced such individuals as Ram Mohan Roy over two centuries ago. We must free ourselves from the anti-Vedic dogma of Radical Universalism that has so weakened Sanatana Dharma as a world-view and a culture. We must re-embrace an authentically classical form of Sanatana Dharma that is rooted in the actual scriptures of Sanatana Dharma, that has been preserved for thousands of years by the various disciplic successions of legitimate *Acharyas* and *gurus*, and that has stood the test of time.

We must celebrate traditional Sanatana Dharma, and we must do so on its own terms alone. The Neo-Hindu importation of Radical Universalism may resonate with many on a purely emotional level, but it remains patently anti-Vedic in its origins. Radical Universalism is an indefensible proposition philosophically, and a highly destructive doctrine to the further unfoldment of Sanatana Dharma. The dogma of Radical Universalism has not attracted more people to the Vedic tradition, as many of its early originators had hoped. Rather, it has kept intelligent people away from the Vedic religion and philosophy.

Chapter Ten: Logical Fallacies of Radical Universalism

Radical Universalism is not a doctrine that we find anywhere in traditional Vedic texts, or taught by any of the classical Vedic *Acharyas*. In addition to demonstrating the non-Vedic nature of Radical Universalism from a historical and literary perspective, however, it is also important to examine the validity of the claims of Radical Universalism from an overtly philosophical perspective. This chapter, and the ones that follow, are the most important chapters of this book because they conclusively prove both philosophically and epistemologically that the central premise of Radical Universalism – that all religions are the same – is an erroneous and indefensible claim.

In order to philosophically assess the central premise of Radical Universalism, we need to see if the propositional statement that "*all religions are the same*" even makes any objective rational sense at all. As we will now see, the dogma of Radical Universalism is riddled throughout with logical inconsistencies, contradictory assertions,[43] *ad absurdum* implications, and self-defeating conclusions. In the following section of this work, I will examine some of the more absurd philosophical problems that naturally arise from attempting to uphold a Radical Universalist

---

[43] Radical Universalism defies disjunctive logic in its very claim that the many either/or propositions contained in the varied mutually exclusive theological statements of a multiplicity of different religions are without meaning. For example, the mutually exclusive claims that the inherent nature of the Absolute is **either** ontological Nothing (the Shunya of Buddhism) **or** ontological Personal Being possessed of an infinite number of auspicious attributes (Para-Brahman of Sanatana Dharma). Logic insists that the Absolute must be one or the other, and cannot simultaneously be both of these contradictory claims. To defy disjunctive logic is akin to claiming that one is a married bachelor or that one is in possession of a square circle. These are either/or propositional statements that inherently cannot be reconciled.

perspective. This will be done via applied philosophical assessment employing both propositional and veridical analysis, as well as original methodological procedures that I have personally developed for philosophical textual analysis.

We're Not Superior…Therefore We're Superior

Looking first at the very statement "*all religions are the same*" itself, we quickly discover our first problematic instance of circular logic. Let us assume for the sake of argument that Radical Universalism is the consensus opinion among modern Neo-Hindus. Modern Neo-Hinduism would then be, of course, the only major world religion that upholds this notion of radical equality. As we know, present day (as well as historically instantiated) leaders of orthodox Buddhism, Jainism, Sikhism, Taoism, Judaism, Christianity and Islam would all vehemently disagree with this statement that "*all religions are the same*". These religions all reject any notion of Radical Universalism. Each of these individual major religious traditions is quite vocal in their assertion that their own unique paths, concepts of the Absolute, and soteriological perspectives (theories on the means to achieve spiritual freedom) exclusively reflect their own idiosyncratic traditions.

More, they would all assert with equally vociferous force that their own exclusive path holds a clearer insight into the nature of Truth, and a surer means for salvation, than does any other faith on Earth. Indeed, if each leader of each specific religious tradition did not believe that their own religion had a stronger grasp on Truth, then to even be a leader of that specific religion would hold no meaning. Why, after all, would someone even be a member of x religion and not y religion if they did not feel that x religion had something to offer that y religion did not? No other major religion outside of modern

Neo-Hinduism teaches that "*all religions are the same*". If Neo-Hinduism does teach the doctrine of Radical Universalism, modern Neo-Hinduism, then, would be the singular instance of a major world religion teaching that "*all religions are the same*".

The problem that is created is that since only Neo-Hinduism is teaching the supposed "truth" that "*all religions are the same*", and since no other religion seems to be aware of this supposed "truth" other than modern day Neo-Hinduism, then Neo-Hinduism is naturally superior to all other religions in its exclusive possession of the knowledge that "*all religions are the same*". In its attempt to insist that all religions are the same, Radical Universalism has employed a circular pattern of logic that sets itself up as being, astoundingly, superior to all other religions. Thus, attempting to uphold the very claim of Radical Universalism leads to a situation in which Radical Universalism's very claim is contradicted. Radical Universalism's claim that "*all *religions are the same"* automatically makes Radical Universalism inherently superior to all other religions! Therefore, all religions are **not** the same. A good way to see the inherent circular logic of this claim is to conduct a formal propositional analysis of the argument.

Radical Universalist Fallacy I

1. Modern Neo-Hinduism is the only religion that supports Radical Universalism.
2. Radical Universalism states that *"All religions are the same."*
3. No other religion states or knows that *"All religions are the same."*
4. Since a) no other religions know the "truth" that *"All religions are the same"*, and since b) only Neo-Hinduism knows the "truth" that *"All religions are the same"*, only Neo-Hinduism knows the truth of all religions.
5. Only Neo-Hinduism knows the truth of all religions.
6. Therefore, Neo-Hinduism is both distinct and superior to all religions.

7. Therefore, given Neo-Hinduism's distinctness from and superiority to all religions: **not** all religions are the same.
8. Since all religions are not the same, therefore Radical Universalism is untrue.

It is clear and apparent that the groundless affirmation of Radical Universalism by lesser-informed contemporary Neo-Hindu teachers leads to an inescapable spiral of self-defeating logic.

In its very attempt to supposedly level the theological playing field by claiming that *"all religions are the same"*, Radical Universalism is automatically compelled to assert its own inherent superiority, and to assign to itself the status of the sole possessor of the "truth" that all religions are the same, thus negating its original claim in its entirety. In essence, what Neo-Hindu apologists of Radical Universalism are saying is: "Since only we possess the knowledge that all religions are equal, then we must be the best." It being the case that Radical

Universalism is superior to all other religions, of course, all religions are then necessarily not equal.

Chapter Eleven: Radical Universalism and Ethical Relativism

A further problem caused by Radical Universalism is that it necessarily leads to ethical relativism. If "*all religions are the same*", after all, then by inferential extension all the various ethical systems taught by these different religions must also be the same. To state that they are not is to undermine the very basis of Radical Universalism's claim, which is that all religions – and by logical extension, all the contents of all religions – are the same. Ethical Relativism is a postmodern, materialist philosophical view that claims that there are no objective, constant or discernable ethical standards that apply to humanity. There is no transcendent spiritual basis, according to the insistence of the Ethical Relativists, or even any categorically sufficient rational maxims, for any comprehensively applicable ethical rules or behavior.

Thus, on Ethical Relativism's account, God is not the author of humanity's inborn, inherent sense of right and wrong; and neither can moral standards be discerned through the power of reason. Ethics, in other words, is deemed to be rooted neither in a transcendent source, nor even in the human intellect. Indeed, Ethical Relativism believes that the existence of any objective moral norms is merely an illusion. There are really no right or wrong actions. There are merely fleetingly subjective rules that apply to a particular individual, at a given time, in a given situation.[44]

Being an atheistic and materialist doctrine,[45] Ethical

---

[44] Another name for this modern dogma of Ethical Relativism is thus Situational Ethics, i.e., the argument that ethics is determined solely by the determining factors of the given situation in question, and not by solid principles that are antecedent and independent of the specific situation then occurring.

[45] From a spiritual perspective, Ethical Relativism would be classified as a specifically Left-Hand Path, or Luciferian (i.e., demonic) doctrine. The Left-Hand Path is not part of the Sanatana Dharma tradition, and stands in direct opposition to it. It is the very opposite of the Dharma perspective on the

Relativism would relegate such religious moral principles as compassion, mercy, justice, truthfulness, trust, loving others, and non-violence to the realm of meaninglessness. It would consequently render any sense of ethical behavior as being without ultimate merit or purpose outside of the purely functional and Machiavellian value that such principles might possess in an immediate and individual given situational instance in time.

When modern Neo-Hindus claim that *"all religions are the same"*, this unequivocal statement also necessarily infers that all actions that are carried out in the name of all religions are similarly equal. After all, if Radical Universalists were to make the assertion that one religion's ethical/moral beliefs are better, or superior, or make more sense than another religion's ethical/moral beliefs, then they are again contradicting their original supposition of

---

question of the nature of ethics.

the radical equality of all religions.

Consequently, what one religion upholds as being morally acceptable must be precisely equal and the same in ethical content and implication to what all other religions uphold as morally acceptable – even if the moral claims of these various religions directly contradict each other. To state otherwise undermines the underlying premise of Radical Universalism itself. One religion's accepted behavioral norms, according to Radical Universalism, are just as legitimate as any other religion's accepted behavioral norms. Since all religions are supposedly equal, then necessarily all religious ethical standards are also equal.

While there are arguably some discernable similarities between some ethical rules upheld by some of the world's many religions, we also find that there is a great deal of dissimilarity between the ethical systems of many religions. When we perform even the most rudimentary comparative analysis of the major world religions' diverse ethical systems, we immediately see that there is some considerable disagreement between them on even the most fundamental question of what is a morally good action versus what is a morally objectionable action.

In some religions, for example, it is considered immoral to drink alcohol (Sanatana Dharma, Islam, Evangelical Christianity). In other religions, by contrast, alcohol is just fine (Judaism and Catholicism). For some faiths, the killing of animals to eat meat is an ethically prohibited activity (Sanatana Dharma, Jainism, and much of Buddhism). In others, killing animals is an ethically neutral activity (Islam and Christianity). In some religions it is considered morally legitimate to periodically kill members of another religion merely for being members of a different religion. Historically Judaism, Christianity and Islam have all been culpable in supporting such a view, to greater or lesser degrees, that it is permissible to kill heretics and infidels. For the vast majority of the other religions of our world [46] - Sanatana Dharma included - on the other hand, to kill someone simply because they practice a different religion from one's own would be considered a demonic and immoral act.

What we find when we comparatively examine the moral teachings of the world's many religions is that, not only is there great diversity of opinion on the question of what constitutes morality, but in fact we often find ethical theories that lie in direct contradiction to each other, and are thus mutually exclusive claims. Some of these ethical theories necessarily reflect righteousness, and some

---

[46] There is a stark divide between two categories of religion. A) Abrahamic religions (Judaism, mainstream Christianity, Islam, and Bahai) versus B) all other, Natural Law (Dharma) oriented religions. It is specifically the Abrahamic religions that endorse violence against followers of other religions. The Natural Law religions do not.

definitely do not. In order to further understand the problem in attempting to ignore mutually exclusive ethical claims, we will use the following scenario.

Live and Let Die

In the following scenario, we have two individual members of two distinct religious traditions. Person **A** belongs to a religion that believes 1) it is morally right to worship iconographic images, and 2) it is morally wrong to kill another person merely due to that person's religious belief. Person **B**, on the other hand, belongs to a religion that states that 1) it is morally wrong to worship iconographic images, and 2) it is morally right to kill another person merely due to that person's religious belief.

Person **A**, a Vedic priest, is sitting by the banks of the River Ganga. He is offering a *puja* (worship ceremony) under the warm, embracing rays of the Indian sun. Before him lays his object of adoration: an iconic *murti* (religious statue) of the Divine Mother. Person **A** is merely performing a religious duty as prescribed by his religious tradition's beliefs and practices.

As person **A** is peacefully offering his *puja*, person **B** rides up on horseback and observes the religious actions of person **A**. According to person **B**'s religion, offering worship to any form of iconic religious image is tantamount to sin; it is an abominably terrible act of immorality. Moreover, in person **B**'s religion, person **B** is morally obligated to end the life of person **A** for worshiping such an iconic image.

Person **B** proceeds to lop off the head of person **A** with a sharp sword as person **A** quietly worships. Person **B** gets back on his horse and proceeds on his journey happily secure in the knowledge that he performed a positive religious duty in faithful accordance with his religion's moral teachings.

In both the instances of person **A** and person **B**, each individual was merely performing his religious duties and following the moral principles specifically ordained by his respective religion. So diametrically opposed to one another were the prescriptions, goals and justifications of these two distinct, religiously inspired moral systems, however, that person **A** is dead, while person **B** feels justified before his god for having killed person **A**. For someone bound by the irrational dictates of Radical Universalism, believing that the paths and moralities of all religions are equal, both actions must be seen as being equally moral.

If a Radical Universalist were to criticize person **B** for his religiously dictated action, then the Radical Universalist would be contradicting his own belief. Of course, person **B** <u>should</u> be condemned for his action by any objective moral criteria that one could ever employ. This being the case, if the Radical Universalist were to stubbornly stick to his stance that all religions, and thus the ethical systems of all religions, are equal, then he is foolishly and smugly justifying evil. A person cannot be a Radical Universalist and yet uphold universal moral principles at the same time.

When the assertion that "*all religions are the same*" is made, it is also automatically inferred that the moral systems of all religions are the same as well – even if many of the rules of these moral systems are diametrically opposed to one another. In supporting Radical Universalism, the ethically barren conclusions of Ethical Relativism are also naturally supported. The consequent results are that moral proscriptions and prescriptions that are otherwise contradictory and mutually exclusive are seen as equally valid – a position that cannot be logically asserted.

To support Radical Universalism is to say that being violent and being non-violent, to be tolerant and to be intolerant, to have compassion and to have religiously inspired hate are all morally equivalent. The idea that there can be moral equivalency of diametrically opposed moral rules is not upheld by any serious religion on Earth,[47] Sanatana Dharma included. The following propositional analytic breakdown will better illustrate the inferential inconsistencies inherent in Radical Universalism from an ethical perspective.

Radical Universalist Fallacy II

1. Radical Universalism claims that "*all religions are the same.*"

2. If "*all religions are the same*", then the moral principles of all religions are necessarily also all the same.

3. This is so since, if some ethical principles

---

[47] The only exceptions to this rule being the pseudo-religions of the Left-Hand Path and Luciferianism, which are not real religions, but actual anti-religions.

are seen as superior to others, then the religion upholding those superior ethical principles is also superior, thus negating the central premise of Radical Universalism.

4. We see that the ethical principles of all religions are actually **not** all the same.

4b. Moreover, we see that some ethical principles upheld by some religions are diametrically opposed to some ethical principles upheld by other religions.

5. To claim that diametrically opposed ethical principles are all valid is to support the moral equivalency theory of Ethical Relativism, which **no** religion does.

6. Therefore, Radical Universalism necessarily entails Ethical Relativism.

7. Since Ethical Relativism is not valid, Radical Universalism is not valid.

8. Therefore, Radical Universalism is not valid.

Or, alternatively stated in syllogistic logic:

RU if and only if ER

-ER

Therefore -RU

To say that "*all religions are the same*" is to also claim that "*the moral systems of all religions are the same.*" In turn, to claim that all ethical systems are correct is ultimately to negate all ethical systems altogether, which is precisely the goal of the pseudo-philosophical project known as Ethical Relativism.

Relativism Revisited

Radical Universalism leads, via consecutive logical sequence, directly to relativism, both ethical and philosophical. Sanatana Dharma, on the other hand, is thoroughly non-relativistic in both its ethical outlook and on the questions of what constitutes reality, truth, the Absolute, as well as life's meaning and ultimate goal. Classical Vedic

Acharyas taught that the metaphysical and ontological truths revealed by the Vedic religion (via the epistemic mechanism and valid means of knowing termed *shabda-pramana*) are necessary truths. Their non-contingency is derived from the fact that they are eternal, trans-material, un-authored and untouched by human fallibility and deceit.[48]

Though admittedly some of the *Acharyas* did have some slight differences in their interpretation of these necessary truths, the revealed truths of the *Vedas* were clearly recognized by all classical Vedic *Acharyas* - without exception - as non-relativistic, transcendent truths nonetheless. The divinely inspired content of the Vedic scriptures are not contingent truths, the truth-content of which might be in any way alterable by either subjective opinion or by empirically mediated disputation. If these

---

[48] Thus, one of the technical Sanskrit terms for the Vedic scriptures is *apaurusheya*, or non-manmade.

truths were merely relative and at the mercy of mere subjective opinion, then their value as reliable philosophical and spiritual guides would be severely undermined. Consequently, the unstable, shifting sands of Relativism, in all its varied forms, has been recognized by countless generations of spiritual teachers as being a baseless and imperfect foundation upon which to base one's search for the Absolute and Perfect (God).

Relativism has been recognized by multiple generations of philosophers, both Asian and European, both Dharmic and even Abrahamic, as being a philosophically untenable position, the logical implications of which naturally leads to its own self-determined demise.

Relativism, in the most general sense of the term, makes the broadly sweeping assertion that *"There are no absolutes"*. The difficulty in attempting to prove this indiscriminate contention is that Relativism is incapable of producing such grand axiomatic statements in such a manner that Relativism itself does not violate the logical rigors of its own statements. The moment a Relativist puts forward the proposition that *"There are no absolutes"*, the Relativist has just committed the error of himself making just such an absolute statement, which is then itself negated by the proposition that *"There are no absolutes"*. Whether speaking in religious, philosophical, aesthetic, metaphysical or ethical terms, Relativism thus neutralizes itself by the self-negating power of its own propositional assertion. As can also be seen in the Relativist dogma of Radical Universalism, Relativism contains within its very own philosophical structure the seeds of its own concomitant refutation.

Chapter Twelve: Sanatana Dharma – The Empty Mirror?

A further self-defeating aspect of Radical Universalism is that it severely negates the very need for Sanatana Dharma itself, relegating the Vedic tradition to merely being an ideological vehicle subservient to the Radical Universalist agenda, and rendering any meaningful sense of Vedic cultural and religious identity barren. If the Radical Universalists of Neo-Hinduism claim that *"all religions are the same"*, then each and every religion is simultaneously deprived of all attributive uniqueness. They are deprived of their uniquely intrinsic identity. This is manifestly true of Sanatana Dharma even more so than any other religion, since if Radical Universalist Neo-Hindus had their way, they would be the sole representatives of Radical Universalism on the world religious stage today.[49]

---

[49] This is, of course, predicated upon the desired procurement

If we say that the ancient teachings and profoundly unique spiritual culture of Sanatana Dharma is qualitatively no better or no worse than any other religion, then what is the need for Sanatana Dharma itself? Sanatana Dharma then becomes the blank backdrop, the empty theatrical stage, upon which all other religious ideas are given the unbridled freedom to act, entertain and perform…all at the expense of Sanatana Dharma's freedom to assert its own identity. The self-abnegating absurdity of a "Vedic" Radical Universalism reduces the Vedic religion itself to a theologically empty shell, a purposeless and amorphous religious entity. The Vedic religion's only individual contribution to the realm of religious history would be to negate its own existence by upholding the teachings of every other religion on Earth, while simultaneously denying its

---

of the long-term Neo-Hindu goal to eventually fully subvert authentic and traditionalist Sanatana Dharma and to eventually have Radical Universalism become the central operative thesis of the contemporary Vedic tradition.

own inherent distinctiveness.

Sanatana Dharma, subjugated to the Radical Universalist agenda, would find itself reduced to being merely an inert mirror, doomed to aspire to nothing more philosophically substantial than passively reflecting every other religious creed, dogma and practice in its Universalist imposed sheen. This is how the problem breaks down from a purely logical perspective:

Radical Universalist Fallacy III

> 1. According to the Radical Universalists, modern Sanatana Dharma is the only religion that purportedly teaches Radical Universalism.
>
> 2. Radical Universalism says that "*all religions are the same.*"
>
> 3. Since no other religion believes this, no other religions are obligated to prove Radical Universalism.
>
> 4. Since only Sanatana Dharma supposedly

teaches Radical Universalism, only Sanatana Dharma is obligated to prove Radical Universalism by its own example.

5. If Sanatana Dharma then attempts to assert itself as a religion that is in any way distinct and exceptional, then it automatically violates the tenets of Radical Universalism.

6. Therefore, if it were to uphold Radical Universalism, Sanatana Dharma must negate its own intrinsic attributive excellences.

7. In negating its own intrinsic attributive excellences in the name of a so-called Radical Universalism, Sanatana Dharma then negates its own *raison d'etre*, its own reason for existence.

8. Therefore, in upholding Radical Universalism, Sanatana Dharma necessarily loses its reason for existence.

Radical Universalism necessarily leads to the destruction of Sanatana Dharma as a comprehensible system of beliefs. Rather than relegating Sanatana Dharma to a shadowy imitation of its vibrantly true self, we must reject the enervating influence of Radical Universalism, and re-embrace the authentic teachings of our tradition. Anything less will necessarily lead to the Vedic tradition's inevitable demise.

Revisiting the Mountain Top

I want to return briefly to the inadequately developed, yet habitually employed, metaphor that depicts the diversity of spiritual traditions as merely being supposedly different paths ascending "the one great mountain of Truth." This is an image that we see repeatedly employed by apologists for Radical Universalism. As a general image of the courage, determination and inner resources necessary to ascend the path to Truth, the climbing of mountains, ladders and stairways are images that we see employed often, and by a wide variety of religions. When this image is used by the various world religions, however, it is always with the understanding that the summit of the given mountain in question is representative of the specific idea of the Absolute that the particular religion has in mind.

The mountain metaphor has never been used by any serious religious tradition prior to the 19th century to express the idea that the summit somehow represents a common goal for all religions, i.e., Radical Universalism. Obviously, since not every religion shares the same metaphysical, theological or ontological conception about the ultimate nature of the Absolute, nor the same soteriological goal in knowing that Absolute, not every religion is trying to climb to the top of the same theological mountain.

There are several radically distinct, and wholly irreconcilable, religiously inspired ideas about what constitutes the Absolute. Consequently, rather than attempting to artificially claim that there is only one mountain top toward which all religions aspire, it would be more truthful, and more in keeping with what the various religious traditions themselves actually say, to state that there are several different mountains – each representing a radically different idea of what is the Absolute.

There is a Nirvana mountain, a Brahman mountain, an Allah mountain, a Jain Siddhashila mountain,[50] a Christian Heaven mountain, a mountain of Tao, etc. Some mountains are monotheistic, some are polytheistic, henotheistic, pantheistic or panentheistic. Some mountains are of the nature of nothingness (*shunya*).[51] Moreover, it is incumbent

---

[50] Siddhashila is the realm to which the most perfected liberated beings in Jainism go to dwell eternally. This is achieved once all material *karmas* are eliminated. "Owing to the absence of the cause of bondage and with the functioning of the dissociation of *karmas* the annihilation of all *karmas* is liberation." - *Tattvārthasūtra* (10.2)

[51] In addition to the fact that each and every religion represents a different ultimate goal and conception of the Absolute, there are, of course, also a variety of sub-sects within each major world religion, sometimes to the extent of there being thousands of such sub-sects. Indeed, within Christianity alone, there are a known 45,000 diverse sects!

upon us all individually to choose for ourselves which of these many possibly correct Absolute-mountains we wish to scale. Each one of these mountains are different and distinct from one another. Only one of these mutually exclusive philosophical mountains, however, can be the correct one.

Three important factors that differentiate the nature of various religions are a) The Problem: an analysis of the fundamental existential dilemma that human beings face, b) The Solution: the proposed soteriological escape from our existential problem, c) The Absolute: the nature of the ultimate Reality. These three factors differ as we compare one specific religion to another specific religion.

(Snibbe, Kurt. *Orange County Register*, April 7, 2023.)

The Abrahamic Mountain

Different religions are clearly aiming at different, most often mutually exclusive, soteriological and theological goals. For the Abrahamic religions of Judaism, Christianity and Islam, the human person is seen as a sinner who is in need of repentance, divine forgiveness and renewal. The soul is born upon conception and does not preexist the physical body. The Absolute for these allied traditions is an omnicompotent, anthropomorphically envisioned, monotheistic god.

The Buddhist Mountain

For Buddhism, on the other hand, it is taught that the human person is unnecessarily experiencing suffering due to mistakenly perceiving himself as an enduring, self-conscious entity. Liberation, in Buddhism, begins with the realization that there is no eternal self (no soul; *anatman* in Sanskrit, *anatta* in Pali), but only momentary states that give the illusion of a permanent person. The final extinction of the human person in the form of *nirvana* (literally "blowing out") is thus the goal. The Absolute is correlated with *Shunya*, the void, emptiness. For Buddhism, there is no God, no soul, nor any other permanent metaphysical reality.

The Vedic Mountain

For Sanatana Dharma, the human existential dilemma is our illusion (*maya*) of separation from the Absolute that is caused by ignorance (*avidya*) of our true state as permanent spiritual beings (*atman*) and our false identification (*ahamkara*) with that which is alien to our true and eternal soul. Our soul is immaterial, eternal, of the nature of pure bliss and awareness, as well as sourced in, and dependent upon, God. Liberation (*moksha*) is achieved by transcending this illusion via Yoga, meditation and following the teachings of the Vedic scriptures, and by realizing our qualitative union (*yoga*) with, and dependence upon, the Absolute. Speaking in the most general of terms, the Absolute in Sanatana Dharma is designated as Brahman. In ontologically personal and philosophically more sophisticated expression, Brahman is known as Sriman Narayana. Sriman Narayana is the omnicompetent, non-anthropomorphic, panentheistic Supreme Personality of Godhead.

The Jain Mountain

For Jainism, the human dilemma is caused by our mistaken notion that we are dependent and temporary beings with limited knowledge. Liberation (*kevala*) is achieved when we realize our true nature as independent, eternal and omniscient beings. For Jainism, there is no God, but rather independently existing liberated persons are the collective makeup of the Absolute. The ultimate goal for Jainas is to become an arihant, a liberated being, and to dwell forevermore in the eternal realm of Siddhashila.

As we can see with these four radically different approaches[52] to the three fundamental issues of a) the Problem, b) the Solution, c) the Absolute, there are many conflicting and irreconcilable contradictions between them. Each of these traditions holds a very different account about what constitutes our true spiritual nature; each has its own distinctive idea of what it means to realize our true nature; each expresses concepts of morals and ethics, as well as actual spiritual practices, that are often diametrically opposed to one another; and each has a uniquely divergent idea of what is the ultimate nature of the Absolute.

---

[52] These four very diverse religious approaches are, of course, only a tiny sampling of the radically irreconcilable beliefs and goals of what are in actuality many thousands of distinct religions, each representing their very own "mountain" of religion.

I have chosen these four broad religious traditions (Abrahamic, Buddhist, Vedic and Jain) to illustrate the point that, not only are there different religions, but there are also different categorical *types* of religion. There are different religious systems to such an extraordinary degree of dissimilarity that the very philosophical premises and conclusions that they each uphold are divergently unrelated and directly contradictory one another. The Abrahamic religions, consisting of Judaism, Christianity and Islam, we can term Anthropomorphic Monotheism. Buddhism we can call non-Theistic. Sanatana Dharma can be understood as Panentheistic. Jainism is Anthropotheistic.

These four categorically different types of religion are wholly irreconcilable, i.e., if the claims of one is true, then the claims of the other three are necessarily false. Religion **A** is a categorically different type of religion from Religion **B** if what must exist if Religion **A**'s problem, solution and

Absolute are correct cannot simultaneously co-exist with what must exist if Religion **B**'s problem, solution and Absolute are correct, and vice versa.

Given the mutually exclusive assertions that each of these four categorical types of religion uphold about a) the analysis of the human existential dilemma, b) the means to human freedom, and c) the ultimate goal to be realized; the overarching feature of all these four distinct types of religion is that, if the philosophical content of any one type is true, then the philosophical content of the other three are clearly not. It is as logically impossible to hold that these religions are all true, or even that any two of these religions are simultaneously true, as it is to say that there is such a thing as a round square, or a married bachelor. Such a nonsensically contradictory proposition <u>can</u> (and very clearly <u>is</u> in Neo-Hindu, Radical Universalists, and New Age circles) be perhaps verbally spoken, but it <u>cannot</u> be rationally thought.

Chapter Thirteen: Brahman – The Absolute of the Vedas

Let us look now at what Sanatana Dharma, specifically, holds to be the nature of the Absolute. The ultimate goal and Absolute of Sanatana Dharma is philosophically termed Brahman in the ancient and sacred Sanskrit language. The word Brahman comes from the Sanskrit verb root *brh*, meaning "to grow". Etymologically, the term means "that which grows" (*brhati*) and "which causes to grow" (*brhmayati*). Brahman, as understood by the totality of the scriptures of Sanatana Dharma, as well as by the *Acharyas* of the Vedanta school, is a very specific and non-replicable conception of the Absolute.

This unique Vedic conception of the Absolute has not been fully enunciated by any other religion or philosophical system on Earth, and is exclusive to

Sanatana Dharma. Thus, to even call this conception of Brahman "God" is, in the technical sense, somewhat imprecise, if only due to the popular misconceptions that have accrued over the centuries in connection with the term "God". This is the case because Brahman does not in any manner refer to the anthropomorphic concept of God of the Abrahamic religions. Brahman is not in any way the same as the object of worship that is found especially in the Old Testament or the Qur'an. When we speak of Brahman, we are not referring to the "old man in the sky" concept that is prevalent within Judaism, mainstream Christianity or Islam. Neither do we refer to the idea of the Absolute as even capable of being vengeful, jealous, vindictive, fearful or engaging in favoring a chosen people from among His human creatures. For that matter, Brahman is not a "He" at all in the strict sense of material, biological sex, but rather transcends all empirically discernable categories, limitations and dualities.[53]

In the *Taittariya Upanishad* 2.1, Brahman is described in the following manner: *satyam jnanam anantam brahma*, "Brahman is of the nature of truth, knowledge and infinity." Infinite positive qualities and states have their existence secured solely by virtue of Brahman's very reality. Brahman is a necessary reality, eternal (i.e., beyond the purview of temporality), fully independent, non-contingent, the source and ground of all things, and the possessor of an infinite number of auspicious qualities and attributes overflowing in abundance to an infinite degree. Brahman is both immanently present in the realm of materiality, interpenetrating the whole of reality as the sustaining essence that gives it structure, meaning and existential being, yet

---

[53] The Supreme Absolute of Sanatana Dharma both transcends all material designations, while also being recognized as a being who is one, yet simultaneously two in the form of Sriman Narayana, Goddess-God, Shakti-Shaktiman. For a much deeper explanation of this aspect of Vedic Divine ontology, see my book *The Shakti Principle*.

Brahman is simultaneously the transcendent origin of all things (and thus is panentheistic in relation to all things).

As the primary causal substance of material reality (*jagatkarana*), Brahman does not arbitrarily will the coming into being of the non-Brahman metaphysical principles of matter (*jagat*) and individuated units of consciousness (*atmans*), but rather they are manifest into being as a natural result of the overflowing of Brahman's grandeur, beauty, bliss and love. Brahman cannot but create abundant good in a similar manner to how Brahman cannot but exist. Both existence and overflowing abundance are as much necessary properties of Brahman as love and nurturing are necessary qualities of any virtuous and loving mother.

One can say that Brahman Itself (more correctly, Him/Herself) constitutes the essential building material of all reality, being the antecedent primeval ontological substance from whence all things proceed. There is no *ex nihilo* creation in Sanatana Dharma.[54] Brahman does not create from nothing, but from the reality of Its own being. Thus Brahman is, in Aristotelian terms, both the Material Cause as well as the Efficient Cause of creation. As the source of Dharma, the metaphysical ordering principles inherent in the design of the cosmos, Brahman can be viewed as the Formal Cause. And as the final goal of all reality, Brahman is also the Final Cause.

---

[54] In yet another of thousands of radical distinctions between the Abrahamic religions versus the non-Abrahamic religions, the Abrahamists believe that creation occurred *ex nihilo*, i.e., from nothing. The non-Abrahamic religions, including especially Sanatana Dharma, teaches that there is no *ex nihilo* creation, but that prime materiality pre-existed enformed "creation".

Being the ontological source of all reality, Brahman is, in actuality, the only substantial Real that truly exists, all other metaphysical categories being either a) contingent transformations of Brahman, having their very being subsisting in attributive dependence upon Brahman, or else b) illusory in nature. These views about the nature of Brahman are in general keeping with the theological teachings of both the Advaita and the Vishishta-Advaita schools of Vedanta.[55]

All reality has its source in Brahman. All existence has its grounding sustenance in Brahman. It is in Brahman that all reality has its ultimate repose. Sanatana Dharma, specifically, is consciously and exclusively aiming toward this reality termed Brahman. Not all religions are aiming at the Vedic concept of Brahman as outlined above. It is crucial

---

[55] Vedanta (*veda* = wisdom; *anta* = culmination) being itself the very highest culmination of philosophical thought available in the Vedic tradition.

for us to have first comprehensively grasped the full ontological implications of the Vedic concept of Brahman in order to clearly understand the fallacious premise of Radical Universalism.

Brahman and Free Volition

The primary reason why Radical Universalists claim that *"all religions are the same"* is due to the pretentious assumption that the various individual Absolutes toward which each religion aims is, unbeknownst to them all, really the same conceptual goal. In other words, Radical Universalists believe that the members of all other religions are also really seeking Brahman…they are just not intelligent enough to know it! As every non-Vedic religion will vociferously affirm, however, they are not seeking Brahman.

Brahman is **not** Allah; Allah is **not** Nirvana; Nirvana is **not** Kevala; Kevala is **not** polytheistic gods/goddesses; polytheistic gods/goddesses are **not** Yahweh; Yahweh is **not** the Cosmos; the Cosmos is **not** the Ancestors; the Ancestors are **not** the Law of Attraction; the Law of Attraction is **not** tree spirits; tree spirits are **not** Brahman.

When a religious Muslim tells us that he is worshipping Allah, and not Brahman, we need to take him seriously and respect his choice. When a Buddhist tells us that he wants to achieve Nirvana, and not Brahman, we need to take his claim seriously and respect his decision; and so on with the claimants of every other religion on Earth. To disrespectfully insist that all other religions are really just worshipping Brahman without knowing it, and to do so in the very name of respect and tolerance, is the very height of hypocrisy and intolerance.

The uncomplicated fact is that, regardless of how sincerely, emotionally and passionately we may wish that all religions desired the same Absolute that we Sanatana Dharmis wish to achieve, other religions simply do not. They, and we, are attempting to climb a multiplicity of categorically different mountains, at the top of which are all mutually exclusive and irreconcilable goals. We need to accept and live with this concrete theological fact.

Chapter Fourteen: Distinguishing Salvific States

Just as the conception of the Absolute is different and mutually exclusive from one religion to another, in the same way, differing religions have mutually exclusive ideas about a) the path to salvation, and b) what is the state of the person upon receiving salvation.

The mainstream Christian's sole aim in salvation, for example, is to be raised physically from the dead on the eschatological day of judgment, and to find himself with Jesus in heaven, who is to be found seated at the right hand of the anthropomorphic male Father/God of the Old and New Testament. Christians are not seeking Brahman. Muslims aspire toward a delightfully earthly paradise in which 72 *houris*, or virgin youth, will be granted to them to enjoy (*Qur'an*, 76:19).

Muslims do not seek the same salvific goal as Christians. Jains are seeking *kevala*, or "aloneness", in which they will enjoy an eternal existence of omniscience and omnipotence without the unwanted intrusion of a God, a Brahman or an Allah. All fully liberated beings, according to Jainism, will dwell together in Siddhashila,[56] a realm that is situated at the very apex of the universe (thus situated within the confines of the material world) in perpetual peace – but again, without a God, or Allah, or Brahman! Buddhists seek to have all the transitory elements that produce the illusion

---

[56] The Jaina concept of Siddhashila corresponds with the Vedic idea of Siddhaloka, the realm of extremely advanced *yogis* and ascetics. The important difference between the two distinct understandings is that, for the Jains, Siddhashila is the very highest destination attainable by any liberated being. It is the highest destination, of which there is nothing higher. For Sanatana Dharma, by stark contrast, Siddhaloka (which, like Siddhashila, is also situated squarely at the apex of the material universe) is only a heavenly way-station for very advanced *yogis* who are still striving for full liberation, but have not yet fully completed their yogic work within the material world. Siddhaloka is not the highest attainable ontological realm for the Vedic tradition. Rather, the highest realm is Vaikuntha, the Kingdom of God, which is fully transcendental to the material world.

(and the consequent suffering) of a false notion of a permanent self (*atman*) melt away, and to have themselves in turn melt away into the nihilism (*shunyata*) of *nirvana*. To the Buddhist, Brahman also is an illusion. Buddhists are not in any way, shape or form seeking either a Christian Heaven, Allah, Siddhashila, or Brahman.

Each of these different types of religion has its own categorically unique concept of salvation and of the Absolute toward which they aspire. Each concept is irreconcilable with the others. To state the situation unequivocally, if a Christian, Muslim, Jain or Buddhist, upon achieving their distinct notion of salvation, were to find themselves, instead, united with Brahman, they would most likely be quite upset and confused indeed. And they would have a right to be! Conversely, the average *yogi* probably would be quite bewildered upon finding 72 virgins waiting for him upon achieving *moksha*, rather than realizing the eternal bliss of Brahman. One religious person's vision of salvation is another religious person's idea of hell.

Chapter Fifteen: My God is Bigger Than Your God

What is especially troubling about the sentimentally driven assertion of Radical Universalism that *"all religions are the same"* is the fact that, in its purported attempt to foster tolerance and the unity of all religions, Radical Universalism itself leads directly to intolerance and blind dogmatism. The overriding concern that any religious person must address is: If Radical Universalism is true, then who chooses which concept of the Absolute is the one toward which all religions supposedly aspire? Let us explore now precisely how Radical Universalism leads to a situation of intolerance.

We have shown that there are several, categorically distinct and mutually exclusive, concepts outlining what constitutes the nature of the Absolute. From the perspectives of reason, logic, theological consistency, and common sense, only one of these concepts about the Absolute can be true. This is the case because with any either/or proposition, any one claim automatically entails the negation of any other contradictory and opposing claim. Repeating this example, if x is either a square or a circle, it must be either one or the other. It cannot be a round square! Similarly, the Absolute either has meaningful existence or it does not exist; the Absolute is either an anthropomorphic entity or it is not; the Absolute is either singular or else it is plural; etc., etc. For any one mutually exclusive concept of the Absolute to be true, the other mutually exclusive concepts are necessarily false. To assert otherwise is to reduce the Absolute to the level of absurdity.

By definition the very term "Absolute" means the topmost, greatest and maximally superlative of all existent things. To claim that there can be more than one "Absolute" is as nonsensical as claiming that there are more than one "best", "greatest", or "most important" in any given category. It is the very grammatical nature of the superlative that there can only be one x superlative. Thus, for Radical Universalism to be true, only one concept of the "Absolutes" outlined above can be upheld. To state otherwise is to claim that there are multiple Absolutes. Which in turn means that there is no one Absolute.

Having thus arbitrarily chosen one concept of the Absolute, i.e., Brahman, Radical Universalists have then made the subsequent claim that this one concept is the only concept of the Absolute that all religions are aiming at, whether the followers of these diverse religions are themselves aware of this or not. This, in fact, is precisely the claim that Neo-Hindus who support the non-Vedic idea of Radical Universalism make. For non-traditional Neo-Hindus who assert Radical Universalism, the arbitrary choice for the "one Absolute" that all religions must be aiming toward - whether these individual religions know and agree with this or not - is Brahman. In so doing, however, Radical Universalists are intolerantly imposing Brahman upon all other non-Vedic religions as their supposed real goal, thus undermining those very same non-Vedic people and their ability to make a conscious choice to worship a divinity separate from Brahman. And they are making this involuntary imposition of Brahman upon all other religions in the very name of tolerance!

Radical Universalism: An Intolerant Tolerance

Radical Universalism, as expressed by modern, Neo-Hindus, would seek to deny members of other religions the right to assert their own religions as unique and distinct traditions, and to assert their own concepts of the Absolute as unique and distinct goals. Radical Universalism would seek to deny non-Radical Universalists the right to believe in an Absolute that is categorically not Brahman. Regardless of how radically different the goal of any other religion might be, whether that goal is Nirvana, Allah, or any other, followers of other religions are told that they are all really aiming at the decidedly Vedic goal of Brahman - whether they know this or not, and whether they want Brahman or not.

By extension, in its attempt to falsely conceal the concrete fact of a plurality of distinct and self-sustaining religious systems, Radical Universalism would deny any non-Radical Universalist religion the very basis of their existence. Jews, Christians, Muslims, Baha'i, Buddhists, Jains, Sikhs, Shintoists and members of other religions insist that they are not following the doctrines of Neo-Hinduism, that they are not worshiping the Absolute of Neo-Hinduism and that they are consequently not Neo-Hindus. By forcing them to accept Radical Universalism, the followers of all of these diverse religions are being told that they have no choice but to adhere to the "one true faith" that Radical Universalism upholds. That one true faith is non-Vedic, Radical Universalist Neo-Hinduism.

To insist on the complete equality of all religions is to deny their inherent differences. To deny the inherent differences of varied religions is to deny them the freedom to have their own beliefs, rituals, goals, and ways of viewing the world. One of the most important aspects of the right to freedom of speech is the right to be able to disagree. In imposing one path, one God and one world-view on all the diverse religions of the world, Radical Universalism denies these religions, and the followers of these religions, their dignity and uniqueness. Radical Universalism ultimately denies the uniqueness of individual persons and their ability to hold divergent – and even contradictory – philosophical and theological opinions. It denies us our freedom to respectfully disagree. Fascinatingly, and sadly, in its attempt to force tolerance and equality, Radical Universalism enforces bigotry and an inferior status against any who would dare to disagree with the specific philosophical mountain of Radical Universalism.

Radical Universalist Fallacy IV

1. Radical Universalism proposes that *"all religions are the same."*

2. All religions are not the same, but are actually very diverse in opinion, structure, history, values, ethics, philosophy, soteriology, ontology, goals, etc.

3. Radical Universalism is true if and only if (t ↔ s) all religions are the same.

4. For Radical Universalism to be true, then all religious diversity must be denied

(t ⇒ d).

5. Therefore, Radical Universalism denies all religious diversity.

Chapter Sixteen: One God/Many Names – An Exegetical Analysis of Rig Veda, 1.164.46

Proponents of Radical Universalism have frequently attempted to uphold the dogma that "*all religions are the same*" by appealing to one of the most misunderstood and misused *mantras* in the history of modern Neo-Hinduism. In the *Rig Veda* there is a famous verse (1.164.46) that states: *ekam sad vipra bahudha vadanti*, "God is one, despite sages calling it by various names". For several generations, a variety of Neo-Hindu leaders and practitioners have misquoted this verse *ad nauseam* in an attempt to prop up the dogma of Radical Universalism with a seeming reference to the Vedic scriptures.

Radical Universalists would maintain that this verse is directly pointing to the notion that the ultimate aim of all religions is one and the same, despite the fact that these different religions might call this "one supreme Truth" by many different denominationally inspired or linguistically dictated names. "Whether you call it God, Nirvana, Allah, Brahman, Goddess, Ancestors, Spirits, Elves, Ghosts, rocks, or anything else, you're really only indicating the one supreme Truth" is the commonly parroted refrain of Radical Universalists. Though on a superficially initial glance, this verse of Vedic scripture might appear to be indicating a Radical Universalist viewpoint, when more rigorously analyzed in its proper philosophical and grammatical context, it is clearly saying something entirely different from what modern Radical Universalists contend.

Categorical Exegetical Analysis

In order to fully appreciate the proper purport of the verse *ekam sad vipra bahudha vadanti*, we need to understand the verse in terms of its own inherently derived meaning, and not merely in accordance with polemically determined speculative opinion. We can only do this by explicating the verse in accordance with the verse's precise categorical status, followed by an accurate veridical assessment of its philosophical content. In order to more precisely understand the philosophical meaning of the many verses found in the Vedic scriptures, this verse included, I have developed a methodological system of explication that I call Categorical Exegetical Analysis. This interpretive methodology enables its user to more accurately understand the precise meaning of any singular unit of philosophical text from the Vedic scriptures - units ranging from a simple declarative statement to a string of verses to an entire work - and held together by one unitive philosophical or conceptual motif.

Stated briefly, this philo-exegetical method involves three sequential steps. First, we must determine whether the verse in question is making an actual philosophical statement or some other form of statement (poetic, descriptive, historical, narrative, medicinal, invocative, etc.). In the case of the verse *ekam sad vipra bahudha vadanti*, the philosophically propositional makeup of the statement, the obviously philosophical nature of the subject (*sat*, "Truth/God"), and the clearly unitive conceptual pattern of the verse, undoubtedly makes this a philosophical statement. Second, we need to determine which category/categories of philosophical subject matter the statement falls under by determining the precise philosophical nature of the textual unit under analysis. Is the verse saying something about ethics, about knowledge (epistemology), about liberation (soteriology), about general ontology or Divine ontology,[57] aesthetics, logic, a theodicy,[58] or about some other aspect of philosophy?

The following are the various categories of philosophical statements under which the verse in question could potentially fall under:

> a) **Ontological** - statements outlining the nature of the being. These are further subdivided into general ontology and Divine ontology.
> b) **Ethical** - statements concerning proper/improper behavior.
> c) **Soteriological** - statements about the means and/or nature of liberation.
> d) **Social** - political, economic and sociological statements.
> e) **Aesthetic** - poetic description and/or theory of beauty.
> f) **Cosmological** - statements on the nature of the universe and physics.

---

[57] Divine ontology, as opposed to general ontology, deals specifically with the nature of God.
[58] Theodicies are proposed philosophical explanations for the existence of evil and suffering in the world.

g) **Cosmogonical** - statements about the origin/creation of the universe.
h) **Epistemological** - statements concerning means of knowing.
i) **Logical** - statements that pertain to the rules or implications of logic.
j) **Sadhana** - statements concerning Sanatana Dharma in applied practice (such as Yoga, meditation, etc.).

Every propositional statement containing significant philosophical content that is found in the scriptures of Sanatana Dharma falls within one or more of these philosophical categories. It is impossible to determine the full scope of the intent of any statement without first discerning which category of concern a statement falls under. This is so because of the commonsensical fact that before we can determine what a verse is saying philosophically, we first need to know which aspect of philosophy the verse is addressing. Third, after completing steps one and two, a proper philosophical explication of the verse can be done.

We will now use Categorical Exegetical Analysis to examine the famous verse from the *Rig Veda*: *ekam sad vipra bahudha vadanti*. An exact transliteration of the verse is:

"Truth/God (*sad*) [is] One (*ekam*), [despite] seers (*vipra*) call (*vadanti*) [it] variously (*bahudha*)."

The typical Radical Universalist attempt at interpreting this verse is to view it, incorrectly, as either an epistemological or a soteriological claim. That is, this verse is usually misinterpreted as either saying that a) God can be known in a myriad of ways, all in accordance with the whim of Man (thus seeing this as a relativist-oritented epistemological statement), or that b) there are many ways or paths of achieving God and liberation from suffering (thus misinterpreting this as a soteriological verse).

It is my contention that both interpretations are incorrect. An interpretive error is committed by Radical Universalists due to not understanding the proper categorical context, and thus the proper philosophical meaning, of the statement. The verse *ekam sad vipra bahudha vadanti* is neither an epistemological nor a soteriological statement; but it is rather an ontological one. It is not talking about the proper derivation of authoritative knowledge (*pramana*), nor about the means of attaining liberation (*mokshopaya*, or *mokshamarga*). Rather, the verse is making a clear attributive statement about the essential ontological nature of the Absolute.

The ontological nature of this verse is clearly known due to the fact that *sat* ("Truth, reality, being, God") is the singular nominative subject, which is then qualified by the accusative *ekam* ("one, unity"). "God is One…". Thus the primary clausal emphasis of this propositional verse is clearly placed upon explaining the ontological nature of *sat* (before consonant-initial endings, the *t* becomes *d*; thus *sat* naturally becomes *sad* in this verse) being a metaphysically unified substance (*ekam* = "one"). The emphasis is not on the secondary supportive clause *vipra bahudha vadanti*. The point of this verse is the ontological unity and integrity of the Absolute, that God is one…despite the fact that this Absolute may have multiple names.

The statement *ekam sad vipra bahudha vadanti* is an ontological statement with God as subject, not an epistemological statement with wise-ones as subjects, or a soteriological statement with the means of liberation as the subject. Indeed, multiple paths of liberation are not even mentioned in the original Sanskrit of this verse at all, leaving even less reason for anyone to misinterpret this as a verse somehow supporting Radical Universalism from a soteriological perspective. In summation, this verse is not talking about multiple paths for achieving liberation (since it does not even mention "paths" at all). It is not talking about various means of knowing God. Rather, it is a straightforward ontological statement commenting upon the unitive nature of the Absolute, that God is one. Thus:

"God is one, despite sages calling it by various names".

Chapter Seventeen: Radical Universalism and Vedic Epistemology

For traditional Sanatana Dharma, unsubstantiated claims to truth, such as Radical Universalism, are not merely to be taken at face value. Whether such claims arise from either within the Vedic context, or from a non-Vedic source, these claims always need to be critically evaluated in order to determine the verity of such declarative truth-statements.

Followers of Sanatana Dharma derive their knowledge of Truth from, as well as live their lives in accordance with, the divine knowledge revealed in the form of the *Vedas*. For knowledgeable and traditional followers of Sanatana Dharma, such concerns as personal ethical decisions, philosophical judgments, the nature of the cosmos, the true history of the world, and the efficacy of spiritual practices (*sadhana*) must be in accord with three specific epistemological criteria. These three are: 1) <u>Shastra</u>: The divinely revealed scriptural guidance of Sanatana Dharma (including the *Veda Samhitas, Brahmanas, Aranyakas, Upanishads, Ramayana, Mahabharata, Bhagavad Gita, Puranas, Dharma Shastras*, etc.); 2) <u>Acharya</u>: Authentic spiritual preceptors who teach the truths of Sanatana Dharma with uncompromising honesty, in accord with an authentic Vedic understanding, who represent a legitimate and truly ancient lineage, and who wholly personify what they teach. Such authentic spiritual preceptors in the past have included such truly great *Acharyas* as Shankara, Ramanuja, and Madhva, among many hundreds of others; 3) <u>Viveka</u>: One's own inherent capacity for intelligent discernment of truth versus untruth, reality versus illusion.

It is only by deriving knowledge of metaphysical, religious and philosophical questions in accordance with these three epistemic mechanisms that we avoid being cheated by either our own internal tendencies toward self-delusion, or by externally sourced false dogmas. It is with unequivocal certainty that, when objectively judged by all three of these traditionally accepted validating criteria, the pronouncements of Radical Universalism cannot be upheld as either scripturally supported, attested by any legitimate Acharyas, or as being logically valid or philosophically true. Radical Universalism, then, in accordance with the above three Vedic criteria for ascertaining the validity of any truth-claim, is to be judged a false and anti-Vedic (*avaidika* or *purva-paksha*) dogma.

Chapter Eighteen: Radical Universalism, Christian Missionaries and the RSS

Despite the utter irrationality of the Radical Universalist doctrine, and the fact that Radical Universalism is completely alien to Vedic philosophy, no other dogma has been as perniciously clung onto in modern Neo-Hinduism. In the following section, we will examine the relationship of the important and influential Neo-Hindu movement known as the Rashtriya Svayamsevak Sangh (RSS) to Radical Universalism. The RSS has been an Indian nationalist movement dedicated to the social and cultural renewal of the national ideal of Bharata. Despite many glaring flaws in its Neo-Hindu derived philosophy and program, the RSS has done much positive work to benefit India in the many decades since its founding. As a Neo-Hindu inspired Indian nationalist movement, the RSS movement has had an uneasy relationship with Radical Universalism since the RSS's very initial stages of development.

On the one hand, the RSS has strived for decades, and in the face of often intense opposition, to create a greater sense of Indian identity and pride among Indian Hindus. Yet on the other hand, most of the RSS's top leaders throughout the 20th century, and now extending into the 21st, have been ardent supporters of the non-Vedic idea that *"all religions are the same."* In numerous private discussions that I have had with many RSS leaders over the years, these leaders would often confidentially admit to me the self-defeating nature of Radical Universalism, stating that the doctrine was upheld only for strategic political reasons. The doctrine is being upheld by the RSS despite the fact that this destructive idea has done more harm to Sanatana Dharma than any other idea in the history of the Vedic religion. However, despite their clear acknowledgement of Radical Universalism's many destructive flaws, top leaders of the RSS have, remarkably, held on to this dogma with greater tenacity than most, and to the utter detriment of Sanatana Dharma's longer-term interests.

It has always been a poignant source of despondency on the part of many traditionalist Vedic practitioners that, on the one hand, many leaders of the RSS inspired Sangh Parivar will periodically attempt to defend Radical Universalistic notions in order to opportunistically showcase the liberality and universality of Vedic culture. But on the other hand, these very same leaders will simultaneously denounce Christian missionaries for converting people from one particular "True Path" (Sanatana Dharma) of Radical Universalism to another particular "True Path" (Christianity) of Radical Universalism. Again, if Sangh Parivar leaders are themselves going to uphold the absurdity of Radical Universalism, then they have no right to complain when Christian missionaries simply convert people from one "valid path" to another "valid path". After all, is not Christianity just as legitimate as Sanatana Dharma according to the Radical Universalist world-view? With these and similar attempts at reconciling two mutually opposing programs, such shortsighted Neo-Hindu leaders attempt to have it both ways on the question of whether or not all religions are really just the same.

Radical Universalism is politically expedient in that it supposedly showcases Sanatana Dharma's tolerance of other beliefs; but it is also privately acknowledged as a subversive idea that harms Sanatana Dharma to its essential core. The RSS leaders' answer to this dilemma is to create philosophical round squares by simultaneously affirming both contradictory claims. We are told that Christianity is just as legitimate a path as Sanatana Dharma, while simultaneously being told that we cannot allow any Dharmis to convert to the "alien faith" of Christianity.

Aggressive and unethical missionary activity in South Asia is a legitimate issue that needs to be addressed and combated by all means available to us – most especially by reconverting Dharmis back to Sanatana Dharma and proactively doing outreach to Christians, Muslims and atheists to bring them to Dharma. Holding to such a contradictory position as outlined above, however, is not the most effective way to stem the tide of unethical conversions in South Asia.

The glaring inconsistencies inherent in such an untenable position reveal even more dramatically both the contradictory nature of Radical Universalism, as well as the damaging effects that this unsound dogma has had on our leaders' ability to discern authentic Vedic teachings from absurdities espoused in the name of the Vedic tradition. With such intellectually lethargic leaders as we had witnessed previous to now, is it any real wonder why the average follower of Sanatana Dharma remains completely bewildered about what Sanatana Dharma actually teaches, and that intellectually inquisitive Indian Hindu youth find themselves so easily lured to other, seemingly more rational, faiths?

The gratuitous irrationality of Radical Universalism has led to widespread theological bewilderment on the part of ill-trained Neo-Hindu leaders, the common Vedic parent, and intellectually dynamic Vedic youth. If Radical Universalism is true, then in opposing Christian missionaries the RSS is only opposing another "legitimate path" toward the summit of the "one sole mountain of truth". If Radical Universalism is false and non-Vedic, then the RSS will have to renounce Radical Universalism, and renew and reassert itself with dynamic vigor as the defender of authentic and traditional Vedic Dharma against the aggressive missionary activities of all non-Vedic religions. If such philosophical clarity were to guide our present Vedic leadership, coupled with the Vedic masses finally taking pride in a religion that begins to actually make sense to them, the very real threat of Christian and Islamic missionary aggression toward Dharmic peoples and culture would quickly fade away in the face of a resurgent pride in Vedic Dharma.

Radical Universalism and Neo-Hinduism weaken the Vedic spirit. Pure and authentic Sanatana Dharma fortifies it. If the RSS and the Sangh Parivar are ever going to be taken seriously by the Indian Vedic masses as a movement of vision, courage and legitimate Vedic renewal, the RSS has to decide whether or not the time has finally arrived for Radical Universalism to be firmly denounced and abandoned. Moreover, the RSS needs to realistically assess the damaging effects of Neo-

Hinduism in its own development, as well as in its effects on the greater Vedic community, and realign itself as a defender of traditionalist and orthodox Sanatana Dharma. The immense implications of this intra-Vedic debate for the preservation of Dharma and for securing a meaningful future for Vedic youth cannot be overestimated. We must preserve Vedic culture and secure a future for Vedic children. It is time for our leaders to stand up and take the lead in this regard.

Beacons of Hope

Fortunately, by no means have all present-day Vedic leaders allowed themselves to thoughtlessly succumb to the mind-numbingly infantile influence of Radical Universalism. Indeed, in the present generation we have been blessed with the sagacious guidance of many truly authentic traditionalist Vedic *gurus* and teachers. These authentic *gurus*, many of whom are somewhat lesser known than their publicity-seeking Radical Universalist counterparts, represent some of the most ancient lineages (*sampradayas*) of classical Sanatana Dharma. They have spoken out compellingly and courageously against both Radical Universalism and the Neo-Hinduism from which it took birth, and have articulated the urgent need for the restoration of genuine and traditional Sanatana Dharma.

Among the few, more consciously orthodox Vedic sects who have openly repudiated Radical Universalism and Neo-Hinduism in recent decades is the International Sanatana Dharma Society (ISDS), which was founded in 1998. The ISDS is a global movement, presently represented by followers in about seventy nations,[59] that is

---

[59] The ISDS has serious followers in every single country of Europe, extending from Iceland to Russia and including every nation in-between; throughout the entire New World, including Canada, America, several South American and Central American nations; throughout Asia, including Japan, India, Bangladesh, Pakistan, Nepal, Vietnam, Burma, Turkey, among others; as well as in Australia, New Zealand and South

presenting to the world the most traditional, orthodox, and *Veda*-based teachings of Sanatana Dharma that is possible at this juncture of the Kali Yuga.[60] It is a movement that is situated within the Sri Vaishnava sampradaya and that adheres to the Vishishta-Advaita philosophical system of the great Vedanta Acharya Ramanuja.

The ISDS has presented the teachings of the *Vedas* and of Vedanta in a way that combines the most strictly orthodox and traditional understanding of this philosophy and religion, while simultaneously interacting with the modern world in a way that employs the language, concerns and intellectual reference of our age in a sharp and Vedically-oriented critique of modernity. The International Sanatana Dharma Society represents the cutting edge, the tip of the spear, in the total restoration of

---

Africa.
[60] The Kali Yuga is the current era in accordance with the Vedic calendar. The Kali Yuga began at midnight on February 18, 3102 BC. It lasts for a total of 432,000 years.

pure and living Vedic culture and civilization today. We need to help facilitate the work of such truly genuine, honest, and authentic Dharma movements as the ISDS if we wish to witness the renewal of authentic Sanatana Dharma.

Chapter Nineteen: Reclaiming the Jewel of Dharma

Sanatana Dharma, the one and only truly authentic Vedic tradition, is a religion that is just as unique, valuable and integral a religion as any other major religion on Earth, with its own supremely unique set of beliefs, traditions, advanced system of ethics, arts and sciences, meaningful and beautiful rituals, philosophy and theology. The religious tradition of Sanatana Dharma is solely responsible for the original creation of such concepts and practices as Yoga, Ayurveda (the science of life), Vastu (sacred architecture and city planning), Jyotisha (astrological sciences), Yajna (fire ceremonies designed to access the higher realms of the gods), Puja (ritual altar worship), Tantra (esoteric techniques of *sadhana*), Vedanta (divine ontology), Karma, reincarnation, meditation, self-realization, etc. These and countless other Vedic-inspired elements of Sanatana Dharma belong to Sanatana

Dharma, and to Sanatana Dharma alone.

These many elements of Sanatana Dharma do not belong to any New Age business or movement, Hippie collective, Theosophical offshoot, or any other modern concocted undertaking that would attempt to dishonestly appropriate these sacred Vedic elements. They belong to the eternal religion of Sanatana Dharma alone.

Though these are elements of Sanatana Dharma alone, however, they are also simultaneously Sanatana Dharma's divine gift to a suffering world. Thus, so many of these essential elements of Sanatana Dharma are now to be found incorporated into the structures and beliefs of many of the world's diverse religious traditions, even if without proper attribution to the original religion from whence these elements arose. Much of the world, both ancient and modern, has appreciated, either with direct acknowledgement or not, the greatness of Vedic ideals. When we make the sentimentally comforting, yet unthinking, claim that *"all religions are the same"*, we are unwittingly betraying the grandeur and integrity of this ancient heritage, and contributing to weakening the philosophical/cultural matrix of Sanatana Dharma to its very core.

Each and every time a Dharmi upholds Radical Universalism, and bombastically proclaims that *"all religions are the same"*, he does so at the dire expense of the very Sanatana Dharma that he claims to love. To deny the uniqueness and greatness of Sanatana Dharma as the very fountainhead of all religion leads, in turn, to a very unhealthy psychological state of self-loathing, a sense of unworthiness, and a schizophrenic confusion on the part of anyone who wishes to consider themselves a follower of Sanatana Dharma.

Radical Universalism leads directly to psychological debilitation, intellectual lethargy, and religious confusion on the part of innocent followers of Sanatana Dharma. This is especially the case for Vedic youth. The negative effects of this debilitating inferiority complex, coupled with the lack of philosophical clarification, that result from the denigrating influence of Radical Universalism are the principal reasons why Vedic parents find their children all too often lacking a deep interest in Sanatana Dharma and, in some cases, even abandoning Sanatana Dharma for seemingly more rational and less self-abnegating religions. Who, after all, wants to follow a religion in which it is claimed that the very basis of the religion is to exult the greatness of other religions at its own expense? The answer is: absolutely no one.

If we want to ensure that our youth remain committed to Sanatana Dharma as a meaningful path, that our leaders teach the Vedic tradition in a manner that represents the tradition authentically and with dignity, and that the greater world-wide Vedic community can feel that they have a religion that they can truly take pride in, then we must thoroughly abandon Radical Universalism.

If we want Sanatana Dharma to survive so that it may continue to bring hope, meaning and enlightenment to untold future generations, then the next time our son or daughter asks us what Sanatana Dharma is really all about, let us not slavishly repeat to them the lie that "*all religions are the same*". Let us instead look them squarely and lovingly in their eyes, and teach them the uniquely precious, the beautifully endearing, and the philosophically profound truths of our tradition…truths that have been responsible for keeping the Vedic tradition a vibrantly living and unique religious force for over 5,000 years. Let us teach them Sanatana Dharma, the Eternal Natural Way.

About the Author

Sri Dharma Pravartaka Acharya is universally acclaimed as one of the world's most respected and qualified Vedic teachers and spiritual leaders of the tradition of Sanatana Dharma. Dr. Deepak Chopra exclaimed in 2002: "*You've done truly phenomenal work teaching the pure essence of Yoga*". In a similar manner, Dr. David Frawley has said about Sri Acharyaji, "*Sri Acharyaji represents the Sankalpa [the will] of the Hindu people and the cause of Sanatana Dharma. I urge all Hindus everywhere to give him your full support, assistance, and encouragement in his crucial work. He needs and deserves our help.*" Indeed, *Hinduism Today Magazine* has proclaimed him one of the top five scholars of Hinduism on Earth.

Sri Acharyaji seriously began his personal spiritual journey over 50 years ago at the tender age of ten when he read the sacred Vedic text *Bhagavad Gita* for the very first time. It was soon thereafter that he began his rigorous practice of Yoga, meditation, *pranayama*, *puja* and many other ancient Vedic techniques of spiritual awakening. He was a full-fledged *sadhaka* (a practitioner of yogic practice) living in the city of Brooklyn, New York!

At approximately twelve years old, he took formal Yoga instruction from Sri Dharma Mittra and Sri Swami Bua in New York City. Only a few short years later, he took on the lifestyle of a fulltime Vedic monk, formally living a life of celibacy, self-discipline and great austerity[61] for close to eight years in that capacity. This monastic training culminated in Sri Acharyaji being awarded the status of *brahmana* (Vedic priest) by his *guru*, B.R. Sridhara Swami, in 1986 at his *guru's ashrama* in India.

---

[61] These were deeply upheld practices that Sri Acharyaji would continue to practice throughout his life even after no longer being an official monk.

He coupled his decades of intense spiritual practice and study with advanced academic achievements, earning a B.A. in philosophy/theology from Loyola University Chicago, as well as an M.A. and Ph.D. in religious studies from the University of Wisconsin-Madison. His entire university career was funded by academic fellowships awarded to him as a result of his scholastic excellence and brilliance.

Explaining to his doctoral advisor in 1995 that "*I don't want to just study the history of religion…I want to make religious history*", Sri Acharyaji dutifully left academia upon achieving his Ph.D. to devote himself exclusively to spiritual teaching and to the restoration of the great tradition of Sanatana Dharma.

Sri Acharyaji occupies his full time teaching Dharma spirituality to diverse audiences. In addition to leading classes, *satsanghas*, seminars and lecturing on Sanatana Dharma widely, Sri Acharyaji is a renowned author of over a dozen authoritative books, as well as a personal spiritual guide (*guru*) to a rapidly increasing following of many thousands of enthusiastic students from both the Indian and the non-Indian communities. Currently, he has students and followers in over 70 nations.

Sri Acharyaji was the Resident Acharya (Spiritual Preceptor) of the Hindu Temple of Nebraska from 2007-2009, which represents the first time in American history that a Hindu temple had ever made such an esteemed appointment. Sri Acharyaji is considered by many contemporary *gurus* and leaders of the Vedic community to be the most cutting-edge, authentic, traditionalist and highly qualified Vedic *guru* in the world today.

Members of the International Sanatana Dharma Society acknowledge Sri Acharyaji as a truly enlightened sage, as a *sad-guru* (true *guru*) capable of guiding his disciples to the deepest realization of wisdom and spiritual liberation, and all members strive to follow his spiritual teachings in our daily lives with sincerity, loyalty and fidelity.

For more information about the life and teachings of Sri Dharma Pravartaka Acharya, please visit his website and consider becoming a member of the International Sanatana Dharma Society:

www.dharmacentral.com

Bibliography

Agarwal, Vishal. "*The Ancient Commentators of Prasthana Trayi.*" Unpublished manuscript, 1998.

Burtt, E.A. "*Types of Religious Philosophy.*" Harper and Brothers, 1951.

Carr, Brian and Indira Mahalingham. "*Companion Encyclopedia of Asian Philosophy.*" Routledge, 1996.

Christian, William. "*Opposition of Religious Doctrines.*" Herder and Herder, 1972.

Frawley, David. "*Arise Arjuna: Hinduism and the Modern World.*" Voice of India, 1995.

Frawley, David. "*Awaken Bharata: A Call for India's Rebirth.*" Voice of India, 1998.

Frawley, David. "*Hinduism and the Clash of Civilizations.*" Voice of India, 2001.

Hardy, Alister. "*The Spiritual Nature of Man: A Study of Contemporary Religious Experience.*" Clarendon Press, 1979.

Larsen, Gerald James and Elliot Deutsch (eds). "*Interpreting Across Boundaries.*" Princeton University Press, 1988.

Lipner, Julius. "*The Face of Truth.*" SUNY Press, 1986.

Lott, Eric. "*Vedantic Approaches to God.*" Macmillan, 1980.

Misra, Vacaspati. *"Nyayavartikatparyantika."* Ed. G. S. Tailanga. Vizianagram Sanskrit Series, no. 9, 1896.

Phillips, Steven. *"Classical Indian Metaphysics."* Open Court, 1995.

Ramanuja. *"Sri Bhasya."* Trans. Swami Vireswarananda and Swami Adidevananda. 2nd ed. Calcutta: Advaita Ashrama, 1986.

Sankara. *"Brahma-sutra-bhasya."* Trans. Swami Gambhirananda. Calcutta: Advaita Ashrama, 1983.

Sharma, Arvind. *"God, Truth, and Reality."* St. Martin's Press, 1993.

Smart, Ninian. *"A Dialogue of Religions."* SCM Press, 1960.

Smart, Ninian. *"Doctrine and Argument in Indian Philosophy."* Allen and Unwin, 1964.

Sri Dharma Pravartaka Acharya. *"Introduction to Sanatana Dharma."* Dharma Ascending Press, 2021.

---. *"Sanatana Dharma: The Eternal Natural Way."* Dharma Ascending Press, 2015.

---. *"The Sanatana Dharma Study Guide."* Dharma Ascending Press, 2016.

---. *"The Vedic Way of Knowing God."* Dharma Ascending Press, 2009.

Thomas, George F. *"Philosophy and Religious Belief."* Charles Scribner's Sons, 1970.

Yandell, Keith. *"The Epistemology of Religious Experience."* Cambridge University Press, 1993.

Yandell, Keith. *"Philosophy of Religion: A Contemporary Introduction."* Routledge, 1999.

Made in the USA
Columbia, SC
23 March 2024